UNCHARTED
LIVES

Also by Stanley Siegel and Ed Lowe, Jr.

The Patient Who Cured His Therapist

Stanley Siegel and Ed Lowe, Jr.

UNCHARTED

LIVES

Understanding the Life Passages

of Gay Men

A DUTTON BOOK

DUTTON

Published by the Penguin Group
Penguin Books USA Inc., 375 Hudson Street, New York, New York 10014, U.S.A.
Penguin Books Ltd, 27 Wrights Lane, London W8 5TZ, England
Penguin Books Australia Ltd, Ringwood, Victoria, Australia
Penguin Books Canada Ltd, 10 Alcorn Avenue, Toronto, Ontario, Canada M4V 3B2
Penguin Books (N.Z.) Ltd, 182–190 Wairau Road, Auckland 10, New Zealand

Penguin Books Ltd, Registered Offices:
Harmondsworth, Middlesex, England

First published by Dutton, an imprint of Dutton Signet,
a division of Penguin Books USA Inc.
Distributed in Canada by McClelland & Stewart Inc.

First Printing, June, 1994
10 9 8 7 6 5 4 3 2 1

 REGISTERED TRADEMARK—MARCA REGISTRADA

Library of Congress Cataloging-in-Publication Data
Siegel, Stanley, 1946–
    Uncharted lives : the psychological journey of gay men / by
Stanley Siegel and Ed Lowe, Jr.
        p.   cm.
    ISBN 0-525-93813-3
    1. Homosexuality, Male—Psychological aspects.   2. Gay men—
Psychology.   I. Lowe, Ed, 1946–   .   II. Title.
HQ76.S49   1994
155.3'4—dc20   93-42800
                                                          CIP

Printed in the United States of America
Set in Bodoni Book

Designed by Steven N. Stathakis

To Joey
For teaching me to trust the world again
                    —Stanley Siegel

For Ducey
                    —Ed Lowe, Jr.

Acknowledgments

The authors wish to acknowledge those researchers, academics, and clinicians who first identified and described the stages of the coming-out process and the formation of a gay identity. Their work provided the foundation upon which we framed our interviews and shaped this book. Notable among them: Eli Coleman, Vivienne Cass, and Betty Berzon; John P. DeCecco, M. Weinberg, Richard Troiden, Gilbert Herdt, Raymond Berger, C. A. Tripp, James J. Kelly, John C. Gonsiorek, Richard Friend, James Rudolph, Kath Weston, John Grace, Charles Silverstein, David P. McWhirter, Andrew Mattison, and Richard Isay.

We are deeply grateful to the many men who endured our probing interviews and shared so much of the pain and triumph of their lives. We can only hope that this book will honor their courage by the impact of its broader message.

We appreciate the assistance of our editor, Matthew Car-nicelli, for his editorial guidance and his enthusiasm for the project, and of our agent Nancy Rose; and of Joey Smith, Phyllis Singer, Eric Beesemeyer, Gillian Walker, Arnold Dolin, John Patten, Hal Freeman, Rick Mitz, and Maryann Palumbo.

Finally, we acknowledge the courage and inspiration of three men who will not see the completed work: Sam Goldsmith, Kal Berkowitz, and my father, Harry Siegel.

Contents

In conclusion, there are no known cures for homosexuality. Faggots have survived Christianity, psychiatry, social ostracism, jail, earth, air, wind, and fire, as well as the pink triangle and concentration camps. Nothing can reckon with you if you can reckon with yourself.

—from JIM EVERHARD,
Curing Homosexuality

Prologue

In 1987, while marching on Washington, D.C., with a half-million other people, I nearly collided with a woman I knew and her nine-year-old son.

My partner and I and an old college friend of his from Vermont had driven down from New York to join in the first National AIDS March, designed to draw desperately needed attention to the increasingly obvious epidemic and to demand a better response from an unheeding government. It was the first time in history such a huge and open demonstration had organized around a medical issue, and the first time I had publicly appeared as what my father might have called a "card-carrying" member of any population of demonstrators, let alone these men and women. The coincidence of my chance encounter with my friend Margaret was all the more surprising because most of the marchers were gay and lesbian, and Margaret was not.

1

A member of the European aristocracy, Margaret had led a manifestly bohemian existence before settling down to embrace wholeheartedly the American family experience. She had been an art historian, a painter, and later a colleague of mine in psychotherapy in New York. A robust, energetic woman with a grand vocabulary and a voracious appetite for ideas, Margaret greeted you wearing secondhand clothing, charmingly layered and sometimes even garnished with mismatched socks. At her dinner parties you were as likely to meet a world-renowned poet, artist, or filmmaker as an eccentric New York street person with a thoroughly inspirational perspective on a subject like the developing obsolescence of marriage, racism, the novel, or money.

Having decided to take a break from the marching and search for a food vendor of some kind, my friends and I were walking in the opposite direction from the throng when we literally came face to face with Margaret and her matching blond-haired, blue-eyed son.

"Margaret!" I exclaimed.

"Stanley!" she sang in response. To the delight of hundreds of passersby whose palpable joy had seemed fueled by the constant repetition of such gleeful encounters, we embraced and moved to the sidewalk, better to reacquaint and chat.

"What are you doing here?" I blurted innocently. I was relatively new at being me, and I must have considered a happily married woman out of place walking hand in hand with one of her three children among a half-million gays and lesbians. That she also was codirecting an AIDS-related family-treatment project did not mitigate my initial curiosity. Mainly I was struck by the sight of her holding the hand of her son. What was she doing here with him? Before she could answer my first question, I asked the second.

"This is my poetic son," she said proudly, with dramatic, tonal emphasis on the adjective rather than the noun. "Poetic and artistic. I don't know in what direction his life will take him, but I wanted him to see the power of this event and of these extraordinary men and women—the diversity, the dignity, the respectability. I want him to acquire and keep a memorable image of these people and of this event, and what it all represents."

I inferred from her polite euphemisms that she was respectfully considering the possibility her son might be gay, an inference she confirmed for me in a much later conversation.

So many times since then I have pondered with incalculable admiration and some wistful envy the possible impact of Margaret's wisdom, the intellectual agility of her simple act of parental generosity, and—in a way that should not be so spectacularly unusual but nonetheless is—her sense of responsibility. She was determined to keep her son uncontaminated by ignorance and its crippling effects, which in its extreme inspires such homicidal bigotry as that required to fuel a gay-bashing assailant.

Within a year Margaret had all but forgotten the scene, but I kept it like an autographed memory and think of it still as a privileged glimpse into the future, perhaps of a time when the categorical majorities of human beings will have a greater understanding and a less charged view of their counterpart minorities, their mathematically inevitable, spiritually indomitable, and fundamentally natural counterpart minorities, from whom they can learn crucial lessons about the new strengths and virtues necessary for the growth and improvement of the species.

Homosexuals natural?

The world is round. Face it.

Humanity's spectrum includes all variations of tall and short, dark and pale, aggressive and passive, scientific and artistic, brilliant and barely educable, and with the majorities falling comfortably in the middle of the parabolic curve, and the minorities drifting off on either side, providing the relative extremes whose existence proves the average and permits its calculation. All that is natural. Homosexuals appear in every chapter of human history, in every language, culture, tribe, class, caste, race, and religion. Homosexuality occurs in nature, quite simply, quite regularly, and, as the scientific community concluded years ago, quite not by choice.

How did scientists manage to conclude this, asks a recent *New York Times* editorial. "The answer seems startlingly low-tech. Basically the same way they concluded that left-handedness is not chosen, through common sense. Left-handers tell us that they don't choose to be left-handed. Aspects of left-handedness like homosexuality almost universally appear in childhood. As Dean Hammer, an author of a *Science* article [linking a genetic marker to homosexual orientation] says, 'All scientists already agree there is little element of choice in sexual orientation. Genes vs. Choice is an incorrect framework. A much better way of thinking about it might be Genes vs. Hormones.' "

In this book, while talking to people who tell us this, Ed Lowe and I chart the life journey specifically of the homosexual male, the gay man. Looking at him from a presumption of his natural innocence and then acknowledging the unnatural barriers to his growth and development, we discover among other things that he enjoys distinct, liberating advantages over the majority and that some of his creative advantages are advanced by the very homophobic, prejudicial behavior that seems most calculated to exacerbate his isolation and self-hatred.

Gay men who develop beyond self-destruction have a singular advantage: they are outside the prejudicial systems.

Ignored and ostracized in turn by the heterosexist community, the gay man in today's society contends constantly with myths about himself and expectations for himself. Conflicting messages from the world at large both force and encourage him to live his life in a unique way, one vastly different, first, from what his family might have expected of him, and ultimately different from what he might have expected for himself.

From the beginning, because of his awareness of his different-ness, and because a gay child may then separate or isolate himself from the world, he also learns to occupy himself, to entertain himself, to find comfort in solo activities. He develops an apparatus for independence, because he really cannot count on anybody. He may in fact design his own world, refashion, remake, reform, and transform it, filling it with whatever beauty and comfort he cannot find in the hostile, dominant world. These adaptive proclivities are the precursors to skills he later applies in more innovative ways to living a more creative life.

Because he is defined as different, a gay child develops a self-consciousness that translates or converts into an uncommon form of self-awareness. Because he always is monitoring himself in relation to the dominant world, he develops a certain carefulness about his relationship with it. Because he is ostracized and criticized, he tends to identify with other, less fortunate people who fall into like categories—underdogs by and large—and develops a kind of compassion and sensitivity deemed unusual, particularly for a man.

Breaking through the defenses while maintaining his integrity and intimacy in a hostile and unsupportive environment is a heroic achievement at whatever level a gay man manages it. What with the impact of society and culture, the risks in developing close relationships, the necessity of creating a new family, the personal psychological process over the life course, the permutations for his mental health, are that much more complicated, but he is that much stronger and wiser a human being for having plodded his way through his uncharted course.

One way or another, the penalty for being born arithmetically exceptional is that the developing gay man is forced to tap exceptional strengths and creativity to cope with his status and the shame the larger society insists that he feel. Evidence clearly suggests that over generations, coping adaptations become encoded as genetic structures. Could it be that creativity among gay men falls within that realm, like the chameleon's sublimely developed palette?

Adversity forces the gay man to develop a creative genius for living. He can take nothing for granted. The behavioral restrictions designed to ensure the mutual safety and security of lifetime heterosexual lovers, for instance, do not exist or do not apply to him. He becomes acclimated to working outside accepted boundaries, outside rules, traditions, and covenants. Fre-

quently carrying that outsider's rebellious daring into his chosen
professional world, he often is on the cutting edge of whatever
field has attracted his energies. In many ways he is a pioneer,
whether in the revitalization of a neighborhood or the creation
of a new industry. The gay man always seems to be prominent
among the leading innovators in art, literature, theater, music,
dance, film, fashion, and even the sciences. In a way that must
strike Madison Avenue image makers as sublimely ironic, he
most closely approximates, in real life, the legendary American
hero, the true individualist, traveling alone, defying convention,
finding his own shelter, cooking his own meals, exploring new
frontiers, making up rules as he goes bravely along.

This book began as a collaborative attempt by a gay psychotherapist and a straight newspaperman to study and chronicle
the development of the modern gay man. After a short while we
decided to present it to the reader in the first-person singular,
because Ed Lowe talked me into revealing my autobiography as
an integral element of the work, since that painful journey had
inspired the book in the first place.

During the collaboration he began to discern revealing parallels between his lifelong efforts to break free from a web of
self-limiting conventions and my struggle against being exiled
from them while creating my own liberating traditions. I saw
them simultaneously.

Raised in different religions, classes, and cultures to pursue
different ambitions and to mature in different societies, we found
ourselves arriving at the same intellectual, emotional, and spiritual destination by different but similarly individual routes. So
the cumulative effects of twenty years of practice in psychotherapy, plus twenty-five years of practice in human-interest jour-
nalism, plus a hundred interviews, seventy extended telephone
conversations, a spate of debates, a life total of three divorces
and several soul-crushing romantic relationships led us to define
in this book a life journey shared in common by gay men, but
also by anybody who dares to challenge the bigotry of convention
and its built-in limitations.

We did not attempt to study lesbians at all, because neither of us is a woman and both believe the handicap fatal to such an enterprise. However, women have contributed significantly to our understanding of the psychological development of people who suffer from oppression. Furthermore, women, perhaps lesbians in particular, are likely to identify strongly with the process herein described, because it is above all else a human process.

Introduction

Disorientation

A predator, misery loves weakness.

I was home in our new luxury co-op on East 77th Street in New York. At my suggestion, my wife and daughter were visiting my wife's parents in Amityville, Long Island, for a long weekend, maybe longer, depending on my health. I had been feeling ill with the flu and had decided to stop resisting and succumb to it, let it run its course.

Once I settled in, the flu hit me like a fallen scaffold. I had been warned: this virus seemed to have a particularly ravenous appetite for the overwrought and underdefended, which I was, and more so than I knew. Flattened in body and spirit, completely alone and sick for the first time in years, with no woman looking after me, I drifted in and out of consciousness and fever,

sometimes barely aware of time and place, sometimes aware only
of dizziness, aching, fatigue, and malaise.

For solace I turned to music. I fell back in bed listening to
a remarkable piece called "Winter" by pianist George Winston.
Its anguished rhythms and dark, melodic drifts vividly recalled
the cold caprice of winter, and I became swallowed up in the
music and the swirling black-and-white world it conjured for me.
The combined effects of real misery, real solitude, and the au-
ditory accompaniment of really vivid music made me sublimely
conscious of the pervasive emptiness in my life; a reality beyond
the flu, beyond the loneliness and beyond the artistry in the
music; an emptiness all three had combined to tap into and
expose in a way that a return to physical well-being, the family
hearth, and the tintinnabulation of the likes of "Jingle Bells"
was not going to conceal any longer. I was miserable, not just in
the bed, in the apartment, in the music and the disease, but in
my life. I was sad, and I was going to be sad after the fickle
virus finished gorging itself on my strength and took another
mate. I was desperately lonely and would be even lonelier the
moment my wife and daughter entered the apartment. I was mel-
ancholy and unfulfilled and would remain so despite the most
joyous efforts of every composer in history.

What had I done to deserve this revelation, this debilitating
knowledge, this reality? How did I get to the precipice over-
looking so immense a void? It made no sense at all. When I
looked back on the path I had taken, I saw no mistakes, no
wrong turns, no self-destructive detours. As a boy, I was a good
boy. I obeyed the rules as well as or better than any other. I was
a good student. I worked hard to become a good man, by every
accepted standard. A good man: honest, upright, smart, ambi-
tious, successful, compassionate, and gracious.

In my zeal to achieve the happiness promised careful
followers of the treasure map to the American dream, I was ac-
complishing every ambition I had nurtured. I had reached what
I privately defined as the zenith of my profession. Not yet forty,
I was Director of Education at the Ackerman Institute for Family

Therapy in New York City. I was writing a regular column on family problems in one of the nation's largest and most respected daily newspapers. I had been associated with two universities and had founded the Family Studies Center on Long Island. I had been married for the past eleven years to a loyal, caring, talented, and attractive wife, and we had an eight-year-old daughter, Alyssa, who was the love of our lives. I had every reason to be the happiest man in the world, brimming with joy, satisfaction, and fulfillment, and I was more unhappy than I had ever imagined possible, paralyzed by an inability to escape the most profound feelings of desolation, emptiness, and despair.

The flu didn't help matters, or so I thought. In retrospect, I now see that the virus that felled me, imprisoned me in solitary confinement, also forced me to realize that I was not making progress toward some goal I obviously had not adequately defined. Perhaps too weakened to mount the herculean efforts I had used to suppress my true self forever, I began slowly and inexorably to confront certain truths I so far had managed to evade.

Whenever I closed my eyes and gave too much of my attention to the drumming inside my head and the kneading pains that rummaged behind my eyeballs, between my shoulder blades, and deep inside my hips, knee, and elbow joints, I curled up in a near-fetal position and strained to imagine gentle hands caressing me, distracting me with tenderness. I conjured the feeling of the backs of fingers touching my eyelids and my cheeks; of soft hands moving down the nape of my neck to my shoulders; of hands riding lightly over my hips and thighs; of soothing, comforting hands reaching down under the covers to touch me, patiently to stroke me to arousal, to draw my blood ever away from the suffering targets of my disease and exchange the pulsating for throbbing, the bloat for tingling, the fever for the warmth of sensual tenderness and quiet passion.

I became aware, alternately with pain and relief, that the daydream most effectively soothed me when the imaginary hands were attached to an imaginary man, not a woman. I also became aware, with both pain and relief, that I had escaped to this kind of sensory substitution before, as a man, as an adolescent, and as a boy, and that the conversion of pain and discomfort to pleasure and warmth had been effective most often and maybe only when I acknowledged that the tender ministrations of my imaginary nurse-lover represented the attentions of a man and not a woman.

This consciousness was not particularly easy to entertain. I strongly suspect that I would have postponed it yet again had I not felt so weakened and wretched. Sometimes when I reflect on this pivotal four days of flu, I am reminded of Ebenezer Scrooge's magical opportunity to view his behavior from a vantage point outside himself. Scrooge was accompanied by a guide, however, and I was alone. Scrooge watched his daytime self behave in an unmistakably appalling manner, one that offered plenty of opportunity for reform in that it offended almost everyone in the universe, even the miraculously educable, dream-walking miser himself. The behavior I reviewed, my own loyal, by-the-book, following-the-rules behavior, was exemplary and appeared to leave no room at all for reform, not even change. Merely inauthentic, it offended nobody, not even me. Its honors simply had left me empty.

Weary from both the sickness and the lifelong charade, I began to reflect more honestly about my life. Without the supporting cast distracting me and the props of success surrounding me, save, perhaps, for my Perry Ellis sheets, I began to ask, "Who am I?" in a way that I had long ceased to employ in reexamining myself, despite my line of work. Interviewing my memory in much the same way as I would have addressed a patient, I began to review my past and recollect the milestones in my life that Stanley Siegel the therapist would have probed in Stanley Siegel the patient.

I am professionally confident enough to know that in short order, Siegel the therapist would have discovered that all of Siegel the patient's milestones marked a distinctly sexual trail, one that the patient steadfastly and dutifully had not followed.

Involuntarily but willingly, I returned to my first remembered erotic feelings, going back to my sixth year.

I am at Fresh Meadows Swimming Pool in Queens on a rare outing with my father. We enter the locker room to change into our swimsuits, me trailing behind him, carefully glancing up from the puddles in the green tile floor to see naked men for the first time in my life.

It is crowded, and I am aware of nothing as much as my own smallness. No other boys seem to be present. Tall and taller men stand, shuffle, bend, stoop, and stretch wherever I cast my eyes. They are dressed, half dressed, and undressed. I see hair: gray, red, brown, and black. I see pencil-point darts of hair soaked and flattened against calves and thighs. I see tufted curls rising from chests and stomachs, and sometimes backs and buttocks. I see thick forests of pubic hair surrounding thick, bulbous penises. I am trying to be careful not to stare. My skin is tingling as I strip off my street clothes.

Spent towels are draped over the ends of benches and from the tops of locker doors, looking exhausted for having served the needs of the giants who flung them. Gentle, almost childish sounds of feet plinking in the shallow puddles contrast with the tremendous, stentorian weight of deep, exotic voices all around, voices murmuring what must be grandly important secrets, voices bursting into terrible shouts of discovery or derision, voices exploding into uninhibited, barrel-belly laughter, as if the owners of the voices fear nothing in the universe.

The steamy air forces into my little lungs the scent of masculinity and power, the combined aromas of sweat, aftershave lotion, shoe leather, and cigars. I am intoxicated and terrified by the sensory assault.

My father and I stash our clothing in a locker and walk together down a lane of lockers, sometimes turning sideways to avoid contact with the men or the doors or the clothing hanging from the doors. I actually feel the proximity of the men in the skin of my upper arms, my neck, and, of all things, in my ears, which feel hot. I follow my father through a sort of tunnel leading to the pool. At its end is a hard, bright archway of sunlight and a blinding, concrete pool deck surface beyond. In my memory of it I feel as if I am passing from a safe and comforting world into a harsh, cruel world that I never will trust as I do the locker room.

From my sick bed, I recalled that I thought about the locker room for weeks. I did not puzzle over it right away in my boyhood mind as much as I tried to re-create it privately in my imagination, as I closed my eyes before falling asleep or while I tried to gather my awakening thoughts in the bathroom of our house, where I would sniff for its memory in my bath towel or distractedly slap my wet feet against the floor to re-create the plinking sounds of the men's great feet against the wet tile floor. One day I might drape my towel over the toilet seat more cavalierly than before. On another morning I might rub my father's shaving cream on my face and savor the scent for however long it lasted.

Almost unconsciously but certainly consistently, I relived the memory in the very rituals I developed for my morning ablutions. Years later, with the help of the flu, I concluded in one of my spasms of lucidity that the Fresh Meadows locker room had become a benchmark memory for me, the equivalent in my private personal history of a baptism. I would return to the Fresh Meadows locker room again and again to comfort myself when I was terrified and terrify myself when I felt too comfortable. Whenever I felt weary, defeated, anxious, or lonely, no matter how ardently or even successfully I pretended otherwise, my mind carried me back to the sensations of serenity and safety I secretly cherished in the unstated truth of my community with men.

As I realized this, ripples of anger stirred in my mind with a barely perceptible rhythm. Although I am sure I felt them, I did not identify them as anger, or as heralding a gathering storm. I wonder, though, if a piece of me didn't already know that if I died at that very moment, I would have died without having lived my own life.

Still in my haze, I rose from the bed and surveyed the prizes and trophies for how I so far had lived: the trappings of prosperity, the portfolio of newspaper columns, stacks of videotapes of successful therapy sessions, each tape labeled so that I could refer to it while lecturing to graduate therapists all over the country; all visible, tangible rewards and symbols, the fruits of having done what I was supposed to do. They all were as comforting and protective to me as a winter coat without the lining now that I was circling in a holding pattern over my identity, poised to see myself finally in a way that I had been denying for years and with anywhere from moderate to moderately miserable success.

I know that at some probably definable point in the four days, I decided to honor the truth about myself that should have been undeniable from as far back as the Fresh Meadows memory, but I cannot recall the exact moment. Its temptations still were followed by almost equally persistent feelings of being wrong, deviant, aberrant, fundamentally unacceptable.

Like a pendulum, I would swing from my loneliness and self-loathing into one or another exciting but nearly lost memory of acceptance and authenticity, and then have the reverie rudely interrupted by harsh condemnations that would send me back the other way, into misery and deception.

Once, while half dozing, I ran headlong in a long ignored, forbidden memory of being somewhere near thirteen years old and masturbating with a beautiful, muscled, slightly older boy, an athlete with whom I must have had absolutely nothing in common except that he evidently felt the same sort of attraction I felt.

I marveled to acknowledge that I must have erased him from my memory for decades. This phenomenon would become a recurring theme: remembering a life episode of monumental significance while simultaneously realizing that I had managed quite incredibly to have forgotten it. How could I have lived through such an experience as a prolonged, experimental, first ever adolescent sexual encounter and have managed to forget it almost entirely?

It happened in Westbury, Long Island, where I lived from age nine to fifteen. I always hated to think that I grew up there, because in fact I passed through a kind of sleep state there, between my formative childhood years in the city and my years afterward in the city. Still, it was in Westbury, I recalled, that I met this older neighborhood boy.

How difficult it was at first to call up mental snapshots of his image from my mind's memory vault. My face buried halfway in my pillow, I tried but could not remember exactly how or why the boy and I got together, especially considering our differences in temperament, our disparate interests.

I did not remember his name.

I recalled that at the time I knew him I was drawing and painting pictures and already had gained some notoriety as a talented artist both inside and outside the junior high school. Both the work and the accolades from the work were a tremendous source of pleasure for me.

So, it was junior high school.

He was a jock, I remembered that. He was older than I by more than a year, possibly two years. Yes. He was fifteen.

I still could not remember where or exactly how, but I recalled that he taught me how to masturbate. Our first incident probably was very innocent, I guessed, since I most likely didn't know anything at all.

Wait.

I was in seventh grade.

He had a basketball hoop in his driveway. He invited me to shoot baskets.

I bet I shrugged, as if to say that shooting baskets was beyond my capabilities. But I stayed and watched him, I bet. I probably told him he was very good. My memory tells me also that he was graceful. My experience since then tells me he probably was intoxicatingly beautiful to me, the way a lithe, gregarious, athletic girl of fifteen might have been if I were somebody else.

He had this very angular body, a really strong chin and jaw.

He was shorter than I but very muscular in stature, and he always seemed to be posturing, exuding a definitive masculinity.

I think he bounce-passed the ball to me and insisted I shoot. When he saw how awkwardly I shoved the ball upward toward the rim, he didn't laugh. He patiently showed me how to make a layup.

Right.

He taught me to come up from dribbling, eyes up, leaning down into my right foot and pushing off as the ball already was rising from the floor, lifting the ball farther as I rose and approached the basket, "laying it up" against the backboard so that it spun into the basket, and so that eventually it spun into the basket time and time again, almost without fail.

I remembered that; and I remembered working up a sweat, practicing the same shot over and over; and I remembered that after the third or fourth time I stopped at his house to shoot baskets and we worked up the same sweat, the suggestion seemed to drift in from somewhere over the roof of the garage that we take a shower.

I don't think he suggested it in words. I think maybe I followed him into the house and upstairs and into his room or the bathroom or both rooms and watched him turn on the faucets and followed him in as he stripped off his sweaty clothes. And I found myself shedding clothing too, and then, at his blithe and innocent beckoning, I found myself stepping into the shower with him, standing with him, close, wearing nothing more than soap and water. There he taught me how to masturbate. There the fondling began, probably first in the form of a lesson. My parents had not encumbered me with terribly ominous taboos about sexuality, nor had I been subjected to any institutional barrage of condemnations about the sordidness of naked bodies or human contact. I must have known, though, that my entire ancestry, my town, and my concentric circles of acquaintances would have condemned me for touching another male. Why else would I have forgotten it?

I do not know how many times we repeated the ritual, in

the shower and out, in the bathroom, in his room, in my room. Before long, shooting baskets was no more than a pretense for our stumbling together into the shower. His mother worked in an office somewhere and was away during the daytime, so we indulged more regularly at his house. My mother always was around, though that didn't stop us. I was willing to risk discovery to continue to do it, because the feeling was so powerful.

After thinking about it for some time, I remembered that my interludes with my basketball friend became my main focus in seventh grade, probably my best subject, certainly my favorite.

As far as I can recall, this also was my first real friendship with another boy, and its progression almost immediately into a sexually charged relationship made certain that no male friendship ever would be quite the same for me afterward. Though I did not know it at the time, every subsequent relationship with a male would mask a sexual tension that would color it in a terribly confusing way, both because of the existence of the other dimension of the relationship and because I would mount such strenuous, subliminal defenses against recognizing the existence of that other dimension.

So, while this episode of my life was very exciting, it also was very threatening, though I would not have known that either. I would only feel it, already having felt, received, and filed away all the implicit messages about the wrongness of my attraction in my emotional and intellectual memory. My first feeling about myself, whenever I allowed my true self to momentarily exist, always would be shame and guilt.

I am convinced that I fell innocently into that initial period of experimentation. I don't believe I knew what homosexuality was then. I don't know for sure that I knew much about sexuality at all. As the year wore on, I learned to allow myself to be excited by the nuances and the subtlety of whichever of my friend's actions I chose to interpret as provocative. I am pretty sure that as he began to discern my interest and my voluntary and involuntary reactions, he also began to enjoy that specific kind of attention himself, and probably let it excite him. Still—however odd it may sound—I don't know to this day if he was gay. Nor have I any memory of ever thinking that I loved him.

I have an out-of-focus memory of the ending of the relationship. Maybe it ended just when it would have stepped to another level. I think it ended because it became something different for him, not because it changed for me. I think I would not have ended it, probably did not want it to end. While it was going on, I was feeling mainly the paradox of the essential rightness of it and the overriding wrongness, the ever present shame and guilt.

Most striking to me, today as well as during the days I suffered with the flu, was the awful miracle of my self-imposed exile into amnesia. How could I have so completely buried my first sexual experience with another human? I still cannot recall his name. How programmed was I by the influences around me to deny so aggressively what I was feeling, let alone to deny myself a natural reaction to those feelings; and then even to disallow my memory a record of the existence of those feelings?

A heterosexual junior high school boy who was lucky enough to shoot layups and then take showers with a lean, athletic, attractive fifteen-year-old girl several times a week for an entire academic year would remember every second of the experience, gladly and proudly and boastfully and maybe addictively, because it would be such a sensuously colossal benchmark in his life. Not only would he not deny it access to his memory, he would call it up, silently and secretly whenever his burdens had momentarily jostled him, when he wished either to comfort or arouse himself; or openly, perhaps even dramatically, for the excitement and entertainment of whoever gathered around the figurative campfires of his life, possibly even women whom he hoped would be aroused themselves by the very possibility of so innocently sensuous an adventure. For a heterosexual boy, the experience would have begun a positive identification with his sexuality and, ultimately, his whole self.

For me, though every second of the experience is analogous, my otherwise seminal relationship began a long and strenuous process of self-denial, a long and ultimately unrewarding pattern of playacting my way through life, of going through the motions, of following somebody else's chart to someone else's destination, and of forgetting almost completely, or repressing the memory of, such validating life experiences as would have helped me identify myself and rejoice in my own identity.

It led me up the road to what appeared to be success— because my chosen way of fighting what I felt to be my illegitimacy was to create a life of measurable legitimacy—but what actually was a lifelong charade up to this point. In my viral misery I recognized myself instead as a triumphantly successful, soul-sick wretch, the proverbial empty shell. Like so many other gays, maybe all of them in one way or another, I had prayed for the capacity to give up who I was and become whomever the larger society preferred me to be. Not only had my prayers not been answered, I was beginning to recognize that they ought not to have been uttered.

As the flu symptoms began to lift, so rose my resolve to greet myself, to discontinue this futile deception, and to take whatever steps were necessary to reach back and become the man I had started out to be, a man who happened by biological statistic and genetic code to be gay. I had to change my life. No alternative existed. Everything else in my life was right, except the life itself, which was all wrong.

I still would have preferred to follow a legitimate path, if any existed. None did, so I had to improvise. I did not for a moment see as an alternative staying in the marriage and having relationships with men too, as if to test a theory or inaugurate a double life. My self-realization was no theory, and I already had tried duplicity, in a sense, by denying myself access to myself. So I knew I would sever our relationship as a couple before I went about discovering and honoring what I had buried for so long.

I did not know that I was not finished recalling forgotten sexual encounters with other males.

After I emerged from my partly involuntary retreat, I picked a time and carefully told my wife as much as I could remember about the experience and my conclusions, about the Fresh Meadows pool, about the boy I had known in seventh grade, and about how profoundly unhappy I was, trying my utmost to live a life that never was mine to begin with. I tried to convey my affection, respect, admiration, and love for her, knowing all the while that she had followed a map too, and that I was brutally and abruptly wresting it out of her hands and tossing it in the trash.

She reminded me that in graduate school, and for several lingering years after, I had had a sustained homosexual relationship with a man. Once again I found myself stunned to rediscover that yet another revealing chapter in my personal history had found a private room in my mind and closed the door on itself.

The man was older than I by maybe as many as ten years, which was much more significant then, when ten years represented half my lifetime. I went home with him the very night I met him and fell immediately into an affair. I cannot say how I would describe the affair, if, for instance, I would characterize it as torrid. I do not remember many of the details, and I will consider it something of a personal triumph when I do. For a couple of years we continued our romance, which I must have compartmentalized in my mind so that while I was attending classes, it ceased to exist, or it existed as if in the pages of a novel I read only while riding the subway. Whenever I picked up the novel and submerged myself in it, it existed as if it were my whole life. As soon as my wife reminded me of the affair, the highlights reappeared as if called up in outline form on a computer screen.

She had even met the man, she recalled. I did not recall.

Somewhere in those years I had been graduated and had taken a job teaching fourth grade in the public school system in Amityville, Long Island, where she was working as a substitute teacher. The affair with the man already had begun to deteriorate. With her emotional support and help, and with a great amount of pain, now that I think of it (after I walked into my lover's apartment one day and found him with another man), I ended the affair for good.

My wife told me that although she tried to deny it, she knew intuitively that someday I would revisit this "side" of myself, as it were, this "inclination" toward homosexuality. She knew it, as I suppose I did, and pressed ahead anyway, according to the larger society's chartered course, as I did. I had learned by my parents' example how to deport myself as a husband and did so to everyone's general satisfaction, up to and including managing the usual marital problems. Sexually, despite some initial struggle, I conducted a sufficiently satisfactory relationship that my wife never complained about it, though I always felt the haunting absence of a deep sexual connection.

Dissolving an ostensibly solid marriage with a good and decent woman required hours of conversations, discussions, and arguments drawn over days, weeks, and months.

Alyssa was eight years old. My wife and I spent a great deal of time talking about her and about the effect a marital separation and/or divorce would have on her and her future. For a number of reasons, at least one of them selfish, I tried to maintain a positive view: Alyssa would be better off if her parents separated. I did not try to convince anybody that Alyssa's happiness was hinged on her parents' happiness, specifically mine, but I did and do hold that she would forever be influenced by a mutual decision to have her father live his life authentically or otherwise. If, having recognized myself, I continued to live as if I were not gay, the deceit would have a negative effect on Alyssa, even if she never learned the truth of it. Deception in a family does not require discovery to have profoundly damaging repercussions.

Those discussions lasted through the winter. I keep a wonderful photograph of our last Christmas together.

By spring, we had agreed in principle, though not necessarily wholeheartedly, to separate.

I did not conduct an affair while my wife and I were living together, but I was not yet out of the apartment the following summer when I fell in love with John, my first real love, my first completely devastating romantic experience.

The result of the choice I made—to leap into the arms of the wrong partner—led to an emotional disaster whose tragic consequences followed me and colored every move I made. But the melodramatic ending of that first relationship so ruptured my life that everything became dismantled, down to the foundations, which was just what I needed. I wasn't aware at the time that my first flat-out, publicly gay relationship was not the beginning of my new authentic life as I had so giddily and naively thought; it was how I burned down the artificial structure of my former life.

Two years after the flu episode, after the protracted discussions with my wife, after the dissolution of the marriage, after the spectacular love affair and its cinematic denouement, I found myself in San Francisco, alone.

During the following year, I entered into the process of getting to know myself, especially through contact with other gay men and their histories in various contexts. I joined an organization of gay fathers. I attended meetings of gay professionals. I frequented gay centers, gay bars, dances, political events, and gay activist meetings. I began to date. At the age of thirty-eight, I returned to the adolescent stage of summoning the courage to ask someone to go out, then sweating through the classic stages of pre-romantic acquaintanceship, friendship, experimentation, and adjustment, then maybe sexuality. I found that I could skip certain stages entirely, though temporarily, and enter instead what should have been later stages, at least in a chronologically linear life, to see what they were like. So I could take a vacation from the awkwardness of, say, dating, and plunge into recreational sexuality, for example, or middle-aged, indulgent hedonism, or potentially long-term monogamous coupling, and return to the awkward dating stage at a later time.

I always would have to go back, though. I discovered— sometimes to my dismay, sometimes not—that eventually, in order to erase or minimize the inescapable fear of having missed a profoundly important step, as if it were a course, or a class, or a game, a prom, a test, a birth in the family, a death, or an important ceremony, I always would have to go back and live through such stages as I had skipped.

I could not get used to it easily, did not even understand what was happening at first. It was like being in an out-of-control time machine that visited the past but in no chronological order. Then, as I learned to drive the vehicle myself, it became more like a temporal tour bus, where the operator could choose what period of development he wanted to visit and then explore that stage until it became frightening, boring, or until he had lived through it to the satisfaction of his total personal development.

I was far from alone in my ignorance and naïveté. To my surprise, and relief, I found many gay men of all ages stumbling just as clumsily as me through all different stages of social orientation: men in their late thirties and early forties behaving in many isolated ways like goofy teenage boys, like randy college seniors, like promiscuous rakes in their freshman years on Wall Street, Madison Avenue, or Broadway, like town gossips, like newlyweds, and like parental, old married couples.

What perfect sense it later made, upon reflection.

How many men and women had I consulted professionally who, shotgun-married at sixteen, had divorced in their late thirties and then scandalized their families by suddenly talking, dressing, and carrying on like teenage boys and girls? Each of them seemed to have skipped a stage of life, survived as well as they could without its triumphs and failures for as long as they could stand it, and then had snapped back to relive and retrieve the lessons from that missing stage. Each seemed to feel that otherwise, he could not ever be satisfied with his life, having not lived the whole of it.

In a much more severe way, the average gay man has bypassed huge developmental sections of his life by the time he is graduated from high school. Gay youths are not entitled to a typically unsophisticated adolescence, during which they can legitimately and openly date while their carefully observant but nonetheless approving parents monitor them from the sidelines, during which they can stumble and fumble through the protocol of social gathering, grouping, pairing, and coupling the way heterosexual adolescent boys do, before they leave the house as young bachelors to sow their proverbial wild oats.

Gay boys cannot learn or experience any of their true social adolescence while they are living in their parents' house; they are too busy hiding from themselves and then from the world of their families. They often are too preoccupied with the discomforts inherent in pretending to experience what they feel they ought to be experiencing. If and when they do test the boundaries of their social adolescence, they have to do so furtively, and without the barely disguised approval and amused coaching from a parent not all that secretly proud. They have to do it at a later chronological stage too, often many years later. In cases like mine, they begin at the age of thirty-eight. In other cases, twenty-one, fifty-one, thirty, forty-three. I assume that many don't begin at all. Instead they live a lifelong falsehood. With them, no doubt, dies their sad, lonely, and secret triumph: by steadfastly being who they were not, they spared their families and friends the disappointment and embarrassment of having to accept them for who they were.

The phenomenon of revisiting aborted developmental stages is not without its unique attractions. In order to repair his past, the gay man must relive it. Once he gets over the strangeness of the idea and accepts that it is neither foolish nor impossible, he may find that the trip itself can be quite exciting. How many times have we heard a heterosexual man exclaim wistfully, "If only I knew then what I know now!" in speaking of his youth, in referring specifically to how much more he might have enjoyed courtship, dating, or sexuality had he entered that arena armed with the wisdom of another ten or fifteen years?

Well, for however unfortunate the reasons, gay men do enter that arena, finally, armed with years of life experience. A gay man gets to live that fantasy, as well as the fantasy, if he chooses, of, say, his seduction of or by an older, more experienced lover;

or an affair with a younger, less experienced lover; or whatever variation best tantalizes the imagination or fits his needs; this, while he is recapturing what he missed trying to grow up according to a heterosexual set of rules.

So my experience in San Francisco was not exclusively painful and difficult.

However, because of the colossal betrayal I had suffered in my first affair with John, it also was colored by intense mistrust, and for the longest time I thought that affliction too was unique to my case. Of course, it was not.

I was possessed of a hair-trigger suspicion of my own feelings as well—after all, who was I now, anyway?—and I was deeply suspicious of other men and what their interest in me might be about. Plus, I still was coming to every situation with an arsenal of rules for living in a heterosexist community. I had developed to a masterful level my sense of responsibility to that community, as well as my sense of discipline and commitment.

None of that applied in my new community.

Responsibility, for instance, so prized in the heterosexual world, is often not prized at all in the gay community, which by necessity favors invention over convention.

It sounds as if it should not make any sense, until you realize that individual responsibility in a society stems from his commitment to the collective need for order and security. Seeing himself as an integral part of the larger society, the individual views his contribution to it as an important, even an essential duty.

But how can an individual summon such a commitment to a society that collectively declares him nonexistent or, worse, a threat, by his very existence, to the community's sense of order and security? Can a person feel dedicated to a community whose security demands his exclusion, and for no discernible reason?

No.

So, within the gay community, accepting responsibility without challenge may be a devalued commodity, sometimes even a subject of ridicule, because it represents fidelity to the needs of a hostile larger society. Telling a young gay man in this society that he should be socially responsible is like telling a ghetto youth that he should be respectful and trusting of the police, that the police officer is his friend. Each of the two orders is designed for the perpetuation of the status quo. The status quo is designed for the oppression, ideally the eradication, or at least the institutionalized ostracism of the person so ordered. The best way an energetic young non-white man can show respect to this society's police is to act like he is a white man, in which case he risks cruel ridicule from both his exiled sub-community and the larger community he is trying so pathetically to placate. The best way an energetic young gay man can act responsibly in this society is to act as though he is not a gay man, in which case he either abdicates a crucial part of his human self for the whole of his life or indulges it secretly, which puts him at constant risk of betrayal, detection, or both, and the bitter public flogging certain to follow.

As a person nonetheless conditioned to be a member of the larger society at whatever the cost, I still was inclined to be responsible. I still was inclined as well to fall in love, as I had fallen in love with John. I soon learned that falling in love in the classic manner is not the commerce in the gay community either. Rather, it is a condition that gay people must work long and hard even to consider, let alone allow themselves, because society has said over and over in many different and cruelly convincing ways that gay people cannot be monogamously coupled, cannot legally marry, and cannot love in the passionate and increasingly deepening way that is analogous to the ideal love relationship between heterosexual people. It is absurd, of course, and gay people know intellectually that it is absurd. Emotionally, however, while every feeling they have is perfectly analogous to the feelings of a heterosexual—which is why they can write, direct, paint, sculpt, compose, and choreograph the dynamics of heterosexual love so exquisitely—they are conditioned to feel that same-gender love is impossible, and that they must abandon any hope of it, must live without it, must fashion their romantic lives around the remotest possibility of its existence, which, for the most part, they then attempt to do.

Ironically, that makes coupling monogamously the ultimate rebellion against the larger society's prohibitions, and some supremely rebellious gay men aspire to and even reach that seemingly traditional level thanks to exactly that iconoclastic inspiration.

But do they reach that or any other level of development in any traditional order? Do they attain any level of fulfillment or personal development according to a chronologically linear pattern, according to a chart, as it were, like that of their heterosexual peers and counterparts?

No.

In the long, sometimes agonizing route to becoming his best self, a gay man does not follow any chart, because none exists. No sanctioned, institutionalized, liturgized pattern for growing up gay exists in the larger society; no clubs, teams, church-connected or fraternal organizations in his community, lend him support or offer camaraderie during his adolescence and youth.

So the youngster who discovers himself to be gay, the young man who realizes he is gay, and the adult who after however long a lifetime of denial finally accepts himself as being gay (and furthermore as having been gay) must create his own map, must chart his own channels, and must interpret his own experiences as intelligently as he can.

Whereas the heterosexual man is coached through life's important transition periods by a legion of mentors, surrogate fathers, friends, and advisers, a gay man invents his own, individual way to evolve and mature in a hostile society that may include his own father among the leading antagonists.

In doing so, the emerging gay man recreates his own life, rewriting all the chapters that the larger society prescribed for him as if he were born someone else and had a perfect right to mount a framed prom photograph on his bureau, or see his betrothal announcement in the local weekly, or vow his romantic fidelity before an altar and in front of a crowd of friends and relatives, as if he had a right to publicly celebrate anniversaries, dress or speak the way he is inclined to, or entertain such dreams and aspirations as cross his troubled mind.

He does not have any of those rights, of course, and long before he admits that he does not, before he confronts face to face the reason why he does not, he somehow knows that he does not.

The story of how a man-child born gay into our society becomes a gay man in our society is unlike any other boy-to-man story in our experience, first of all because it is not in our experience if we are not gay; second, because it therefore does not follow a familiar plan; and, third, because it does not always happen anyway. Or, it happens despite our society's concerted efforts, individually and communally, to prevent it from happening.

Our society almost always aborts or derails the gay man's development early, either directly by oppression and ostracism, or indirectly through the self-hatred and self-limitation that constant oppression and ostracism so successfully incubate and nurture. The gay man's inevitable internalization of society's view of his homosexuality as either a defiantly spiteful preference or a pathological deviation adds to the individual's already percolating fear and hatred of himself. Furthermore, it interrupts, if it doesn't absolutely prevent, a smooth process of growth and self-acceptance. The ostracism and oppression become a part of the person's psychic drama, and the battle goes on inside the individual as well as outside, throughout his entire life, as the dominant society poses new challenges and new condemnations every day.

Within the population of gay men, as a result, exists every level of self-acceptance/rejection, from the gay man who has managed to maintain his self-esteem but on discovery of his sexuality has been fired from his teaching job, to the gay man who retains his administrative rank in the FBI but bitterly despises himself either for his homosexuality or for his lack of courage to acknowledge, accept, and live it. The feelings range from the extremely timid to the extremely strident, from cowardly to heroic. The gay man who finds refuge among his oppressed brethren therefore is ever surrounded by heroes and traitors, saints and sinners of the highest and lowest orders, and every possible variation in between. The tension, uncertainty, need for support and lack of it, are as constant as ambient air.

The human spirit is an indomitable phenomenon, however, especially when challenged, and triumphant gays grow through the pavement in every generation and in every culture, often assuming roles of especially sociological and aesthetic leadership. But where the average straight man practically can stumble through the psychic passages from boyhood to adolescence through adulthood, middle-age crisis, and senior citizenry, a gay man runs cruel psychic gauntlets every day of his life. Thus, our population of gay men includes examples of every possible range of stunted, altered, detoured, arrested, amended, regressive, and progressive development, and every kind of tragic loss and triumphant exception imaginable from so diabolically vicious a process.

Despite the lack of social growth charts containing legends, place names, alternate routes, and milestones of public approval and encouragement, gays nonetheless develop to varying degrees of maturity, encountering along their meandering way certain common experiences and working however assiduously, or evolving however painfully, through certain identifiable, developmental stages that can be categorized under three major headings.

The stages differ severely from those required for the maturation of a heterosexual man, first in that they are not chronological, because the gay man is not permitted chronology in his growth. Instead he is discouraged from even acknowledging his earliest recognizable gay identifications and impulses. Nor is there a linear order to the stages; one stage of growth does not necessarily arrive after or precede another. No rules exist for passage from one to the next, nor is passage from one required for entry into another. Some people spend a lifetime temporarily testing one stage or more; some jump from one stage to the next in abrupt and seemingly inexplicable ways that outsiders would view as pathologically unstable; others become fixed in one stage and either for security or out of terror never progress beyond it. Yet the developing gay man, almost as in a mythological journey, must master certain difficult tasks and overcome formidable obstacles in order to complete each stage.

Furthermore, in the absence of ceremonies or liturgical milestones marking a sojourner's goals or signifying his achievements, no credibly definable rules exist for behavior at any stage along the way, so that the range of behavior is limited only by the creative limitations of each individual and such ethics as he can invent for a given occasion.

Not all participants complete the journey, though many may appear to have achieved a certain maturity, especially to outsiders irresistibly drawn to pass judgment based on their own maps, which do not apply. Not all gay men even begin the journey; some live whole lives in hiding, either from themselves or from the larger society, or from both. Many gay men who are living as if they did complete the journey actually have vaulted over stages whose revisiting might heal or fulfill them, though they do not know that, because nobody with any authority can tell them; so few wise, old gay men exist to teach.

To the degree that they are divisible, the stages of a gay man's development toward a mature identity fall into certain categories. The structure presented here, gleaned from interviews conducted specifically for this book and filtered through twenty years of clinical practice in psychotherapy, is at bottom an elaboration and expansion of the observations of three researchers in particular. They are: Vivienne Cass, author of "Homosexual Identity Formation: A Theoretical Model" which appeared in *The Journal of Homosexuality*, spring 1979; Eli Coleman, whose paper "The Developmental Stages of the Coming Out Process" was published in *A Guide to Psychotherapy with Gay and Lesbian*

Clients in 1985; and Betty Berzon, author of *Permanent Partners* (1988), who so eloquently presents Vivienne Cass's developmental model.

Our framework evolved as shown:

TURNING POINTS
Pre-emergence
Self-acknowledgment
Self-identification

COMING OUT
Assuming a Homosexual Identity
Accepting Homosexuality
Celebrating Self-expression

MATURING
Reevaluation and Renewal
Mentoring

The first two stages, pre-emergence and self-identification, have a deeper chronological foundation, because gay men often can trace their "different-ness" to early childhood, as early in their memories, for example, as my own reminiscence of the sensory experience in the Fresh Meadows pool locker room. Otherwise, during the course of his life, a gay man can enter and exit any of the stages from the earliest years of his life as a boy to his last years as a man.

Researchers have found that in childhood, whenever memories of homosexual proclivities reach back that far, there exists evidence of a preconscious awareness of a different sexual orientation, both in the individual's mind and in the minds of older observers, members of the individual's family: parents, siblings, aunts, uncles, grandparents, and cousins. The child himself feels different, feels that he is different, feels different from the way his friends act like they must feel. It does not take long for him to begin to feel alienated and/or alone, which feeling is exacerbated by his inability to define or even perceive what exactly are these differences (since no language for them exists).

His alienation from within then precipitates behavior on his part that encourages alienation from without, so that as the rich get richer, the lonely become lonelier, the distant, more distant.

The gay child usually communicates his undefined conflict in the form of some behavioral problem, or through a variety of symptoms, psychosomatic illnesses, or, in extreme cases, a desire to kill the conflict within the self by killing the self. We do have five- and six-year-olds who want to commit suicide for no other apparent reason but that they are different, and we do find out, as they grow, that they are gay, and that their once undefined sexuality was the root difference upon which they recall their childhood depression as having pivoted. Between twenty and thirty percent of gay youths have made suicide attempts, according to the best available statistics (G. Herdt, in *Gay and Lesbian Youth*).

Typically, because the conflict is so powerful, explains Vivienne Cass, the child develops *adaptive strategies* to manage the crises, some deliberate, most unwitting forms of denial, repression, sublimation, and rationalization, that keep him and the family from experiencing the crisis. The adaptive strategies expand throughout his life development. In the early stages, he uses these strategies for managing the feelings of being different and the consequent pain of being an outsider. As he grows older, he becomes more deliberate and less unwitting strategically, making more conscious choices about how to handle the crises his homosexuality continues to present. In the middle stages, as he begins to accept his homosexuality, he more consciously adapts to crises created by ostracism and stigma. He will enhance his own sense of well-being by deliberately employing adaptive strategies that align him increasingly with the gay community, and decreasingly with the community that has clearly begun to shun him. Sexual and romantic experimentation and exploration help him identify himself with others in his new community; forming families of choice allows him both to separate from the very nucleus of the hostile larger community and accept the assistance and support of his own community; changing his

definition of homosexuality erases some of the effects of universal
ostracism and condemnation, allowing for the development of
pride and the celebration of self-expression. This expanding rep-
ertoire of adaptative strategies, which he continuously reevaluates and renews as he encounters new challenges, can prepare
him for the later stages, including parenting, partnering, the
equivalent of mid-life crisis, and the attainment of old age.

But the salient result of this first stage—*pre-emergence*—
in a gay life is that as the feelings begin to emerge, and with
them the growing awareness of "difference" by both the emerging
self and the first concentric circles of the self's acquaintances
—his family and his family's closest friends—so too do the first
efforts emerge to hide or conceal the damnable news, the unspeakable possibility of homosexuality.

In most cases the emergence of the "different" self is followed so closely, so immediately, and so diligently by the
campaign of voluntary and involuntary concealment that the
identity of every gay man in our society is almost by its own
nature cloaked in disguises from the very beginning.

From the earliest of the closeted gay man's experiences and
throughout his life, his mechanisms for concealment become paramount in his arsenal for growth. Consequences of this survi-
valist inclination to conceal roll off and beget new consequences,
from week to week and year to year, each set of consequences
escalating in type, intensity, and craftsmanship as the individual
grows older and more clever.

He begins by concealing parts of himself from himself; the
duplicity eventually rewards him with lowered self-esteem for his
cowardly deceit. He becomes depressed because of his low self-
esteem. The depression intensifies the need for concealment,
since he associates his self-esteem with the hidden, awful, de-
pressing truth about himself. Further concealment continues the
cycle.

Paradoxically, it is during this stage of growth and development that, while isolating himself out of self-protectiveness
and then dealing rather creatively with his undefined conflict,

the gay child often becomes exceptionally independent and self-reliant, often developing as well an intensified passion for creativity, which allows him to amuse and entertain himself without conflict.

Further, because he always is in the throes of an emotional conflict, the gay child forces himself to pay fierce attention to his emotions in a way not required of a child who senses correctly that his feelings almost always are acceptable to the society around him. He becomes especially aware of his and of other people's feelings, and ultimately he earns a reputation for being particularly or unusually sensitive and attentive to the feelings of other people.

The major challenge confronting the gay individual focused in his own emergence is to face the fact of his different-ness, to somehow break through the defensive concealment and denial and become aware of his same-sex feelings without—to the extent that he can make the separation—applying any judgmental projections about their meaning. Children living through this stage almost never accomplish this resolution, but it is an identifying conflict that forever yearns for resolution.

I visited this stage at six years of age and tucked the memory of it under the pillow of my consciousness for life. I encountered it again in seventh grade, when I splashed and frolicked in its frothy surf, but then I ran away to forget as much about it as I could. I visited my emergence again as a graduate student and again hid from it and buried its memory. Finally, at thirty-eight I began to open my eyes and view my own existence.

Like a reader of a Toni Morrison or an Alice McDermott novel that defies temporal rules, a gay man keeps finding himself in events that seem like they ought to have been prior events; he follows himself, entering what should have been chronologically prior stages, where he has to encounter and deal with feelings that seem like they should have been felt long before, should only be memories of prior feelings, long ago wounds, ancient euphoria. The trajectory of his life keeps going backward and forward, sometimes simultaneously. If in his forties he finally accepts himself, he eventually faces the reality that he cannot really establish a wholeness about himself until he goes through his teens as who he is now, rather than as who he thought he ought to have been back then.

Hence the very befuddled and confused behavior of many gay men so often criticized for acting like teenagers. In a way, they are teenagers.

Self-acknowledgment begins once the individual—child, adolescent, adult—realizes what all these emerging differences add up to, these differences that he has perceived between himself and most of the people he knows. Once again, it may not happen until puberty; it may not happen for decades after puberty. It may not happen.

Usually, though, he already is aware, to varying degrees, that he has felt soothed by same-sex romantic fantasies and has felt drawn to same-sex eroticism. Now he is beginning to suspect that the events—in his imagination, in his memory, and in his life—are not merely spasmodic but somehow fundamental. They are not illusionary, not temporary, and not inclinations over which he can exercise very much control. Moreover, the feelings do not visit him because he is desperately, psychologically ill, as he might once have believed, or possessed by some mystical, evil force, as he might once have feared. Hopefully, he accepts —often after a painfully gradual process—that he feels different because he feels different, and that maybe he therefore is different because he is different. He acknowledges that he feels homosexual probably because he is homosexual.

He now is "out," at least to himself, which often is more than half the battle. For a child raised with a psychic gun to his head at all times, self-acknowledgment is one heroic accomplishment.

"Coming out," or announcing the acknowledgment to the public, can be, and more and more frequently is, at least a symbolic culmination of dealing successfully with the first stages of development, but it can be suspect too. Complicated by how internalized is the individual's negativity about himself, a premature public announcement, which is to say, a pseudo coming-out, can easily be a form of self-flagellation or self-humiliation, can simply and innocently be premature, as premature as the wedding of a nine-year-old. In most cases the gay man is dealing with so much negativity from his own immediate outside world, combined with whatever quantity of that accumulated condemnation he has subconsciously embraced as a true definition of his wretched self, he postpones his own self-acknowledgment and self-disclosure as long as he can.

Whereas the task in the so-called earlier stage was to face the existential crisis of being merely different and then break through the defense barriers both known and unknown, the problem here really is to begin the process of *self-identification*, wherein he would change the definition of homosexuality to include himself for the first time and initiate the long, arduous process of self-acceptance, which to a great extent depends on external validation, a rare gem in a hostile world. Since self-acceptance and external isolation don't mix well, and in fact fight each other, the struggle endured by the gay man visiting and revisiting this chapter of his development is one constant, titanic battle against the temptations of self-loathing. Self-identification requires his constant diluting the acidic connotation of what he has learned about the category of homosexuality in order to render even conceivable that he might belong to it. Those who survive at all, let alone triumphantly, generally develop a tremendous inner strength in the process, a self-concept tested by betrayals, rejections, and disappointments and forged by loss and grief. The individual loses constantly—the opportunity to follow convention, the rights to conventional rewards, alliances, loyalties, and support systems that others take for granted.

The gay man cannot take anything for granted, or anyone. But that forces him to develop his own way of navigating his life. So, in this period of *assuming a homosexual identity*, where the individual is aware of his homosexual feelings but only barely ready to label himself, he summons the courage to begin the process of telling others who he is as a way of validating himself, bravely, and in spite of the antagonism from the world around him.

If the growth process was linear and chronological, this stage would be roughly the equivalent of adolescence and early adulthood, wherein the individual would have his first major social and sexual experiences with people who imitate the dominant society by being or pretending to be jubilantly open about their sexuality. It is comparable to adolescence only in terms of the mission, though, not the timing. There almost always is a discrepancy in the timing for a gay man, because there are no sanctions and approvals for his exploring his sexuality when everyone else is, during chronological adolescence.

This is a stage in which the gay man becomes open about his sexual identity and in which other gay people tend to respond in kind. He develops the skills to meet and socialize with people who are visible—which can be especially difficult in the more isolated, more politically conservative suburbs. It is a period of strengthening one's identity and self-confidence as a gay man, though it is fraught with incongruities and terrifying discomforts, especially for a man who is older and who has developed a respectable maturity in all other disciplines save for his true sexuality, where he must yield to the reality that he is a high school freshman.

Visiting, living in, and/or surviving this stage requires courage and enough emotional stamina to carry the individual from giddy to morose and back without making a wreck of him. It also boasts all the elements of adolescent and only slightly post-adolescent sexuality, complete with excessiveness, self-destructiveness, and high risk, much of it intensified by the incongruity of the experience.

It also does involve the repeated realization of fond fantasies, however, sometimes the actualization of fantasies that the participant never dared imagine until they presented themselves in real life.

Putting a positive spin on it, the individual is in a magical position of returning to an unlived past and "knowing then what he knows now." In terms of feelings and the language for them, in terms of general sophistication, he has a much better handle on his self-consciousness in many ways, and in the ways that happen to count most for an adolescent. He is less likely to be absolutely inappropriate, and if he is, he is more likely to be self-forgiving, because he already has dealt with much more shame and ridicule than mere social inappropriateness can match; also, because, since there is no permission to do this, no support, no real rules whatsoever, the individual tends to be more adventurous, exploratory, experimental, and to learn more rapidly the details of who he is and who is the object of his affection. Since there are no gender rules either, he develops a versatility about roles and sexuality. He can be the suitor or the sought. He can offer to do the wash or cook, or both; he can take the garbage out and change the oil. He is not confined by adolescent sex roles because he never was allowed in them anyway. He was queer. Now he is free to be queer.

After a period of sexual and social experimentation, exploration loses its glow, and intimacy becomes more important, writes Eli Coleman. The individual wants to learn how to function in a same-sex relationship in a society where the norm is opposite sex.

Having gone through the adolescent experimentation and literally exhausted his curiosity about what he might have missed, the maturing gay man develops a need for emotional support, connectedness, and human fulfillment. Meeting the need will mark the stage of *accepting a homosexual identity*. However, he still is severely handicapped by a lifetime of isolation, a history of feeling wrongheaded, and a world that simply does not move one centimeter toward rendering same-sex coupling in any way acceptable. He has few if any role models and not much reason to apply to his life the social rules for heterosexual coupling. His parents can't think of any happy, faithful old gay couples celebrating their fortieth anniversaries, and the gay man is ever skeptical, if not suspicious, about monogamous commitment anyway.

Gays become very inventive about how and why they couple. When they do, the reasons often tend to be different from the motivations of heterosexual marrieds. The relationships and the powerfully familial ties that emanate from them are based more on mutual trust and freedom and less on traded vows and enforced exclusivity. They make commitments more to each other and less to the idea of commitment, so when the arrangements begin to fail to serve the needs of both, or all, parties, their loyalties remain with the participants rather than with an institution whose liturgies they were disallowed anyway. They thus develop their families of choice out of the exchanges they have made of trust and loyalty to individuals in their ever expanding concentric circles of friends, acquaintances, and lovers.

Having progressed from the covert world of previously dreaded homosexuality to a social world of gay life supported by a family of choice and a surrounding community, the gay man presses for his full legitimacy, openly confronting prejudice and bigotry, marking his entry into the stage of *celebrating self-expression*, feeling proud of himself, his new family, and his new world. He is willing to be authentic now, in every circumstance, and eager. He may even become an activist or an advocate, or both, separating himself almost entirely from the heterosexual community for such time as he needs to master his anger and then develop a more realistic view of the society around him and the conditions of his life. As he continues to develop, he grows beyond the gay versus straight mentality that served him so well in previous stages and begins to accept that heterosexual people exist who do support him. He now can approach the world more deliberately than reactively, which allows him to begin the process of integrating his homosexual identity with all other aspects of himself. His personal and public identity in all its complexity can become consolidated into a single self-image.

This reintegrated gay man now can enter the parallel developmental track with his heterosexual peers and either suffer or indulge the unavoidable life crisis of *reevaluation and renewal*. He pauses now to question the direction and progress of his life. He takes inventory, reexamines his value system, reviews his triumphs and failures, and either proceeds along his chosen path or changes direction.

Recommitted to life, an experienced veteran of many battles with convention and its often irrational champions, he enters a period of deep self-acceptance and proud contentment. He is a retired soldier, having achieved a life of integrity wherein he has learned to value himself, depend on himself, and survive in the face of stigma, ostracism, rejection, and even hatred. With this genuine wisdom he turns and applies his generosity to younger members of his community, offering the fruits of his experiences, as he enters and enjoys the ironically traditional stage of *mentoring*.

Despite differences in culture, generation, and ethnicity, people respond to prejudice, oppression, and stigmatization in remarkably similar ways. Coming out in the fifties, seventies, or nineties certainly is not the same, nor is coming out at the age of fourteen the same as coming out at forty-five, though the adolescent may be looking toward a long future and the man at mid-life may be reconciling time passed with an awareness of a limited future. Both generations face a similar psychological trajectory composed of necessary developmental crises that must be mastered to achieve a positive gay identity and life of integrity and satisfaction.

No doubt the struggle is less difficult now than it was in the seventies, when gays and lesbians were virtually invisible and there were few social institutions to support their struggle. For that generation, "passing" was its best adaptive strategy. For today's youth, "passing" is considered maladaptive, or at least politically incorrect. No doubt the experience of growing up in the suburbs or in rural communities is more difficult than in urban centers, where there is an active, manifest gay life, including opportunities for open socialization. No doubt the dual identity of being African-American, Asian, or Latino and gay presents extraordinary obstacles, considering the high degree of homophobia within both communities and racial prejudice against them in the predominantly white heterosexist and gay communities.

We are an amazingly diverse community, and how we handle each developmental stage of growth will differ with individual history and culture. However, the stages of growth and development remain constant, and will as long as we are a minority in a predominantly homophobic society.

TURNING

POINTS

For a gay boy, safety is an illusion. Alienation and rejection replace the sense of protection, comfort, and belonging to which childhood ought to entitle him as his different-ness becomes increasingly apparent and begins to disturb both him and those who encounter him. His different-ness throws his childhood off balance, and the resultant fall from innocence is only the first of many turning points that leaves him struggling through his years. He regains his footing only when he answers the questions: What am I? and Where do I belong?

First, he develops a language to describe his different-ness, and therefore the means to think the unthinkable. New knowledge threatens his legitimacy. Out of the threat and the confusion it brings, he has to choose strategies for how he will behave with the knowledge that he is different. With experience he begins to answer the question, to know who he is, what it means, and what are the consequences of its meaning to his family and his society.

At this juncture he must change the connotation of the category *homosexual* in order to belong to it. Otherwise, he will believe he is so hateful as to merit only self-destruction. Once he challenges and conquers what he has learned about this category, he can identify himself to himself as homosexual, though acknowledging it is not being it—not yet.

Pre-Emergence

Growing Up on the Edge of Difference

I never will forget the first time someone called me a fag.

I was at a party. I must have been in sixth or seventh grade. I hung out with a clique of kids with whom I felt fairly comfortable, all of them pretty smart academically, none of them terribly athletic or rebellious. Any one of them could have blended in comfortably with any of the splinter groups that were just beginning to take shape, as if in preparation for the social divisions of high school, which in those years and for the next three or four that would matter most to me included three main subdivisions: the "greasers," dressed in pegged pants and pointy-toed Italian shoes; opposite them, the "collegiates," who wore madras shirts, khaki pants with a buckle in the back, and penny loafers, often without socks; and, somewhere in between, the "surfers," who, though their ranks contained elements of each extreme, managed to look down upon both of the other two groups, as if on top of being cool, athletic, sexy, tan, and handsome, they also knew some poetically intellectual secret of the universe.

The party occupied the kitchen, the screened-in patio, and the backyard of a house in suburban Westbury, Long Island. I thought I would be vaguely familiar with everybody present, or at least that they would be familiar with me. My crowd had been attending school together long enough for our individual idiosyncrasies to have blended with our personalities in such a way that they were, if not unnoticed, at least rendered unremarkable by our group familiarity. Nobody ever had made any remarks, anyway. None that I had heard.

But kids had been invited to the party who were not classmates of ours and who clearly were surveying the field of personalities for the first time, taking scrupulous note of such distinctions as indicated strengths, both admirable and avoidable kinds; and weaknesses, both the insignificant and the exploitable kinds. I had barely stepped out onto the patio, my waxed-paper cup of Coca-Cola in hand, when a snide-looking fourteen-year-old simply said, "Hey, faggot. Are you a real faggot faggot or just a regular mama's boy faggot?"

The suddenness of so unprovoked an attack to an unsuspecting ego must compare analogously to the physical effects of being picked off by a sniper. I remember the feeling of instant heat in my neck and ears as I realized and then accepted that he was referring to me. I felt I was supposed to say, "Fuck you," or "Your mother," or one of the other more generic retorts of the day, but my systems had stopped working, and I could barely raise my head to look at my unsolicited tormentor. I also knew without looking that his friends now were looking at me and were on the verge of laughing out loud. My chest tightened, my mouth dried up. I probably paled, just to make matters worse. If I had fallen down, as if shot, I might have converted the moment to humor, but humor was not my weapon in the first place, and falling down was a maneuver my involuntary musculature already was contemplating.

"Faggot" was an idea I had not had about myself, but the word and the acid soaking it must have exposed a raw, emotional nerve ending of mine, a sort of a visceral suspicion. I knew I was different, but I did not know that the difference might be that I was a faggot.

I left the patio for the yard, hearing the older boy's laughter echo above the din of the party no matter where I stepped, and in so doing I felt as if I had attached a sandwich board to myself and that everybody at the party was stopping to read it. As if suddenly I remembered something I had left in my car—though I had no car, of course—I retreated to the house first, and then lingered in the kitchen, where I realized that there was not enough room at the party for me and my shame. I sneaked out of the front door as quietly and unobtrusively as I could. I didn't have a ride home, but I couldn't bear to ask for one or ask to use the phone so early in the festivities. I walked home, about two miles. When I got far enough away from the party house, I stepped into the leafy sanctuary of a vacant lot and cried. I walked, crying, for what seems in my memory like an entire evening, though I am sure it was no more than fifteen minutes or so. I do not remember any moment in my childhood as devastating or humiliating. I wanted never to see any of them again, the strangers or my friends. I felt bathed in shame, tarred by it, my chest tightened by it. I remember thinking, "Is that it? Is that what I am?" as I tried in vain to pull myself together.

Obviously, there would be no returning to the party, maybe not even to the crowd, or to school, if I could have gotten away with it; and I could not think of any other place to go but home. When I arrived, I still was so innocent about the idea of being a faggot that I told my mother what had happened. Her response made me feel as if the very floor beneath me was collapsing. Out of nowhere, out of no reference I could uncover or recall, she asked, with the bluntness of a hammer to the forehead:

"Well, are you?"

Her tone seemed to have been marinated in anticipatory suspicion. A kick to the groin would have been less of a surprise to me and would have offered me more hope for recuperation.

And, Jesus, was I a fag?

And then, why was she asking me? Does your mom ask you what you are? She had been my mother since before I was born. Wouldn't she of all people know what I was? Was she, of all people, asking me if I was this apparent aberration?

I didn't know what a fag was, really. I had not conceptually put it all together yet. I suppose that night marked the beginning of my beginning to know who I was. I had so far learned mainly that the derision so palpable in the other boy's condemnation of me was in some profound and ugly way reflected almost equally in my mother's partly accusatory, partly resigned tone, when she had converted his declarative statement to her interrogative "Well, are you?"

It felt as if I had just learned that I was adopted and, worse, that at some crucial time in my future my adoptive parents might disavow any knowledge of me, might say: "Him? No, he's not really one of us. He's, you know, a fag."

As far as I was concerned, "Well, are you?" was a question about me from a stranger. Would her allegiance fall more sympathetically with my tormentor than with me? It was as if she had been waiting for me to confess a crime of which I so far was merely totally ignorant.

It also served as my formal welcome to the homophobic world. As far back as I could remember, I had suspected and then had known that I was different. Now I knew what the difference might be, though without knowing what a fag was or what a fag did. I knew only that whatever it was, it was so shameful, my mother was poised to align herself with those who would mock and condemn me for being it.

How remarkable is it that in the centuries of modern history, throughout every culture, within every caste, country, congregation, neighborhood, occupation, profession, trade, class, or clan, we otherwise rational human beings invariably find a representative percentage of homosexuals and still consider their existence an aberration? Every one of our gods has salted every one of our groups with gays—from continents to Cub Scout packs—whom we then have condemned as existing against the laws of our gods.

Gods must sit up nights, shaking their heads in frustration.

In most cultures, though not all, same-gender sexuality has frightened heterosexual populations into a negative emotional reaction so exaggerated as to have virtually eliminated the intervention of any debate on the subject by so threatening an element as common sense.

After all, what dangers to a community has the always present population of same-gender lovers ever demonstrated to people who prefer the more common bond? What exactly is so threatening? Does homosexual desire among men especially present a threat to the conventional arrangement of power and authority, or power and identity, in our society?

Very possibly.

Homosexual attraction illustrates an evidently indomitable tendency for the species to continue reintroducing individuals who periodically will shatter the power theorems of the society and the integrity of the traditional concept of the dominant male self. Homosexual sexual coupling violates institutionalized prejudices. Humans have long known about homosexuality among them and among other mammals; the virulence of the heterosexual population's mass opposition to homosexuality among humans has ever varied, suggesting by its wave patterns a more political than biological origin of the antipathy. Homosexuality among other mammals never has bothered anyone very much, unless as the owner of a gay beast, he was poised to profit on the promiscuity and/or the progeny of, say, his stud. The grandest and most potentially expensive scare in generations of horse breeding happened when Triple Crown-winning champion of champions Secretariat appeared so inordinately shy during his first weeks of employment as a sire, he inspired a spate of rumors within the racing industry that he might be gay. But nobody made any moral judgment about it, nor did they suggest that Secretariat suffered from an overprotective mother.

Otherwise, the very symbolism of male sexuality may be at the root of the mass homophobia in our society. According to Frank Browning, author of *The Culture of Desire*, phallic penetration by men of women happens to be a fair representation of the social position of the genders throughout most of human evolution, a choreography of consistent patterns of power and subordination, rendered most crudely and graphically, but most tellingly as well, in our cruelest curses. "Fuck you" is an imperative whose tone and therefore intent speaks of sexual aggression and power designed to inspire fear and trembling. "Get fucked" or "Got fucked" is our accursed wish for, or our lamentation of, subordination and powerlessness.

In our development so far, being penetrated (the word choice speaks to a passive perspective, as opposed to the more active notions of enveloping, receiving, welcoming, or absorbing) requires a self-imagined passivity associated with yielding, with relinquishing power over the self, with succumbing to a more powerful and empowered person or force. Our collective symbolism grants the male of the species penetration not only of the body, but of the penetrated person in her entirety, body, mind, and spirit, "requiring and permitting therefore entry into the most private domains of the self.

"Marriage, the most prevalent social ritual governing people, provides sanction for penetration . . ." of the body and all its attendant symbolism, writes Browning. "It confirms intimate and public power relations through which individuals and society protect and insure the future." It also perpetuates roles which, especially in the modern era of exponentially advancing societal changes, gradually are becoming less relevant. Size, strength, and other historically crucial physiological gender differences hardly matter anymore. Either party to a heterosexual union now can provide the food and shelter for the entire family, or now can push the requisite buttons that either wash the dishes or fire the air-to-ground guided missiles from the national fighter craft.

A gay man (deprived of the public sanction of his often progeny-less but nonetheless committed marital union) also subordinates his power and pleasure to the gay man who enters him, but by an act of will that is, first, amendable, subject to an opposite act of the same will on another occasion; and, second, not at all an acquiescence to a presumptuous and depersonalizing dictate of the larger society. In fact, it is in open defiance of the larger society.

"Actually, by celebrating his own penetration, the male homosexual offers himself as both an actual and symbolic sacrifice," says Freudian literary critic Leo Bersani, to the notion of usurping the institutions of the society, which may be the root of the society's terrible fear of him. According to Bersani, his desire to be penetrated (the passive voice revealing the traditional perspective) or to receive, absorb, or envelop his lover (the active voice inverting and thereby revolutionizing the perspective) threatens the power position and the authority of the heterosexual male. Gay sex has subversive, symbolic potential, for it offers a genuine model of pluralism and male-female egalitarianism to a society that resists equalizing power and thereby altering the traditional structure to catch up to the advancing technological and philosophical shifts in human behavior.

Skeptics who argue that changing from the passive to the active voice is a trick of viewpoint should consider, first, that adhering to the passive voice, when speaking of the receiver as "being penetrated," is the same trick, and one good trick deserves another. In a relationship between two people, viewpoint and perspective constitute half the perceived reality.

The gay child's undeveloped homosexuality appears at first to be much less of a factor in his emotional well-being than how other people perceive who he is or what he might become. The emotional and psychological development of a naturally gay child is far more dependent on and subject to outside influences than those from within. By statistical representation, he is born into a minority community that is not present to support him when his mental health, emotional development, and self-confidence most require its assistance: in the earliest stages of life. In a way that is totally unfamiliar to a heterosexual participant or observer, the gay child is born with varying degrees and levels of hostility and isolation, and his responses to these unnatural challenges constantly percolate as he adapts and redefines who he is throughout the non-chronological stages of his life.

Although sexuality does not define all of what children do while they are in the nursery, then in the kindergarten playground, it does affect what they do and, to a greater extent, does define who they are. And they know who they are.

In the approaching, if not the arriving, post-hysterical age, it should not—at least upon reflection—seem too outlandish a notion to the heterosexual population that the gay child almost always knows, and much earlier than the larger society has shown a willingness to give him credit for knowing, that in a profound and fundamental way he is not the same as the majority of the children in his family, room, group, playground, school, community and, ultimately, world.

Every child goes through a stage of feeling different. Being a child, he quite innocently feels what he feels and does not question it. Some gay boys tend to identify with other boys and engage in traditionally male, gender-congruent activities. They are accepted by others as gender appropriate, though when they reflect on it as adults, they may recall feeling especially driven to spend time with, play with, and emulate other boys. Their feeling of difference is vague and undefined, and their confusion is more severe for its mystery.

The more obvious gay boy is the one who acts on such inspirations as he feels to play with dolls, try on his mother's makeup and clothing, and participate in traditionally female childhood activities, to the extent that observant adults and even other children notice the difference between his behavior and that of other boys.

The more female-identified child, in the process of being defined as different, becomes aware of the observers' perspective and the reasons for it. He then internalizes the view and begins to feel decidedly different and uncomfortable about it. In a 1981 article on sexual preference, researchers (A. P. Bell et al.) reported finding that homosexuals were nearly twice as likely as heterosexuals to report feeling different from other boys during grade school, and that the source of feeling different "was gender-neutral or gender-inappropriate behavior, or both."

As one gay teen put it, "I always thought of myself as a boy, but I liked doing girls' things. I remember at the age of five or six going into my mother's closet with my sister and my little brother, who also turned out to be gay, and putting on my mother's shoes and dancing around the closet. I think I knew it was not the way other boys were playing. My father certainly knew. My father let us know in so many ways, but without any doubt, that what we were doing in my mother's closet was silly in almost a disgusting way, and very wrong for its silliness. He made it very clear that it was much more wrong and much sillier than other childish things we did. Until then I think I was just having fun, as kids do. I didn't feel bad until my father let us know that there was something especially wrong with that, with what we were doing there."

Many male-identified gay males later will recall that by the time they entered elementary school, they knew that they preferred the company of, and even the affection of, other boys, and in a sexually role-identifying way and, increasingly, in a pre-pubescent, sexual way, so that they even recall having made the more gender-aware girls jealous.

Peter remembers growing up on a military base, just being one of the kids involved in all the expected male-related activities organized for children on base, from baseball to war games. He never remembers a moment when he questioned the male ethos perpetuated by the military that was so much a part of his life. He cannot recall playing with dolls, other than GI Joe figurines, or any other cross-gender activities, though he remembers becoming sexually active at a very early age, including a vivid recollection, with exquisite detail, of a sexual experience with another boy at the age of six. Peter remembered that the difference he felt between him and the other boys was the power of the drive that he felt to be with them and near them, which he now believes was a primitive sexual attraction.

In other cases, an older gay male will remember how as a child he preferred to play the same role as, and enjoy the social acceptance of, the little girls of his society, and how other members of his family and extended family noticed it. Vincent remembered both.

Vincent, fifteen, who recently told his mother that he was gay, tells a story of being caught wearing his mother's makeup and clothing. "First of all," he said with a gently petulant effeminacy, "when I was around eight years old, I liked guys, not girls, and I knew it. My uncles used to ask me if I had a girlfriend, and I used to make up names—Maria, Marianne. I used to think I was weird, in a way, that it's not, like, natural to like guys. It's weird. I thought it was natural, but I knew it was not natural. I remember I told my ten-year-old cousin once that I wanted to be a girl when I grew up. I wanted to be a blonde and change my name to Victoria. I was eight at the time."

For Vincent and others like him, the feeling of different-ness actually is a genuine reaction to a gender incongruity. This gay child is constitutionally and demonstrably different, but he is not constitutionally ignorant, and since the difference manifests itself in behavior that quite simply does not look the same as the behavior of other boys who are not gay, he soon knows that he is different. Stigmatization affects him earlier and more obviously than it does a male-identified gay boy, who does not yet recognize that he is going to be viewed as bad or wrong until later, when he has a language to make the connection between what he feels as his different-ness and the dreaded category of homosexuality. He will escape much of the ostracism because of his gender-appropriate behavior, but eventually find himself more alone when he discovers a definition for his feelings. Because he will have "passed" for so long, he won't even feel an initial kinship with the more easily identifiable gays with whom he eventually will want to align and associate himself.

More relevant than who is the object of these first feelings is the gay child's certitude of the different-ness of the feelings, and the manner in which his family reacts to whatever are his outward expressions of this different-ness. Their relative approval or disapproval determines how easy or difficult, accelerated or retarded, will be his development and growth into his best adult self. For a child, the first expressions of who and what he is are innocent, especially if nobody, including his loved ones, has yet bombarded him with condemnations sufficient to completely convince him of the wrongness of his different-ness. For many, the behavior nonetheless meets soon enough with varying (sometimes astonishing) degrees of rejection, ridicule, labeling and name-calling. This prevailing cultural ethos has the most profound effect on the psychology of a child and on the way he then socializes.

Shame is the first feeling in the face of rejection and isolation by family and peers, for being and/or behaving differently. Having prevailed as emotions, the feelings of inadequacy, inferiority, humiliation, and guilt now merge as shame and become permanently imbedded in the gay individual's feeling about himself. He is bad, or wrong, or damaged, or evil, or inadequate, or freakish; he senses that he does not meet his loved ones' expectations either for them or for himself. He has failed his family and himself, though he does not yet know what he is that is so damnable.

Some gay boys learn this much sooner than I did. Others don't figure it out until they are older. The background music in their minds repeats the same refrain, however. Aren't you ashamed of yourself? Shouldn't you be ashamed of yourself, whoever and whatever is your self?

Members of the dominant heterosexual population, parents react to the child's different-ness first by comparing him unfavorably to siblings and other children who fit the conventional pattern. These parents already have been taught by their parents, to whatever degree they are thereby convinced, that gays are sick, sinful, trivial, even dangerous, and that being gay is one of the most shameful conditions known to humankind. Even the most well-meaning parents then transmit that information to their gay child with whatever degree of conviction they themselves have embraced, or whatever fears they harbor. Moreover, if they also have embraced with similar unconscious enthusiasm the opinion that they have somehow caused the aberration, and that they alone possess the power and the responsibility to prevent or reverse it, they then may behave toward their child, as well as toward each other, either with guilt and shame, or with anger and blame. In classic form, the mother blames the father for being aloof and distant from the "different" son, while the father blames the mother for being so protective and sheltering as to have smothered the boy with her coddling and turned him into a sissy. The child is never unaware of this debate, these feelings, and he often feels responsible for the disagreement. So on top of feeling wrong merely for being who he is, he develops feelings of guilt for causing his parents such shame and consternation over who he is.

"I knew I was different," said another adolescent who spoke of hiding his homosexuality to protect his mother and himself from his stepfather, "because I hung out with girls and knew all the girls' games, like the clapping games. I have six older brothers. They never said nothing except that they thought I was crazy. Ever since I was eight years old, my mother had me going to counselors. She always thought there was something different about me, and we both knew, without saying anything, that if my stepfather thought I was gay, he would kill me. I'm serious too. He would've killed me for being gay. That's the way he felt about gay people. He was a very old-fashioned, tough man. So my mother never told my father about the counseling."

Interviews with gay men and gay teens strongly suggest that the gay child's awareness of his special and moreover unusual attraction to other boys emerges as early as his heterosexual playmates' awareness of their pre-romantic attraction to members of the opposite gender.

As heterosexual boys and girls naturally feel individually drawn to one another, and as they experiment with gender roles and their relative attractiveness in play groups and classrooms, gay children too just as naturally feel their own preprogrammed, magnetic pulls. In many cases they even recognize simultaneously both what they are feeling and that it apparently is uncommon among their fellows; it is different.

Traditional psychoanalytic theory holds that the first erotic fantasies a heterosexual boy entertains are about himself in a relationship with his mother. Its corollary suggests that the first erotic fantasies a gay boy entertains involve his father as a romantic partner. According to the doctrine of repression, adult gay men withhold from consciousness the actual erotic feelings and fantasies about their fathers from their early childhood, screening them behind recollections of feeling different. The theory thus reduces the depth and breadth of gay men's remembered experience to a buried, erotic fantasy. If, however, modern researchers prove correct, and homosexuality is genetically or biologically based, then the memory of feeling different is much more than a mere smokescreen. It is instead exactly what gay men report it to be. It is as profound as people report feeling it is. It involves all of the human systems in interaction, not just the erotic.

Almost every gay male harbors at least one vivid early-childhood recollection of feeling what he sooner or later realized was a same-gender erotic or sexual and therefore homosexual attraction. The men I interviewed recall, and I do as well, early feelings of this "special" attraction toward another male, one that often mirrored in its tenderness the similarly romantic reminiscences by heterosexual boys and men about a particular girl in their nursery school and kindergarten classes. It seems to me that what gays (and heterosexuals) do recall is far more significant and revealing than what they don't.

Watch toddlers at play. Their first romantic fantasies are

barely fantasies at all. They hug and fawn over each other, paw and coo at each other, yawp and stare at and then pine for each other in ways that cause their mothers to swoon with romantic intoxication over the adorable scene being played out before them—unless, of course, the character pairings are not appropriately heterosexual, in which case the mothers smile wooden smiles and scoop up the noncombatants for suddenly remembered next appointments.

Some of the openly gay adolescent males I interviewed recalled these feelings and realizations from as far back as ages four, five, and six, and could also recall that they soon recognized that what made them different was not only gender-based but sexual, and that it was fundamental. Now knowing what sex was, they had observed (second) that most boys liked girls the way most men appeared to like women, and (first) that they liked boys that very same way.

"I remember at about age seven or eight," said one gay adult, "we would watch *Dr. Kildare* on television every week. The feeling that I felt for the character was very different from my feelings about anybody else. I now recognize or identify them as feelings of romance and desire. I had no language for what I was feeling then, certainly no sexual language. I remember wanting to be private with him, to have some special communication that would be more than friendly. I wanted to be important to him, sort of like his boy but not his son."

At some point between fantasizing about and the unrequited longing for the tactile affection of an unrelated other person, and his first truly romantic sexual experience, a boy learns about masturbation and—if he learns from another boy, as some do—about sex play. Boys whose family, ethnic, religious, and cultural backgrounds make sex play an unspeakable sin learn about masturbation through a process that their own maturing bodies inaugurate for them, beginning with nocturnal emissions, "wet dreams," and, more specifically, beginning after they awaken in the middle of a few. Pubescent, sexual experimentation is a very private, personal and often troublesome experience for such boys, because though it affords them the luxury of privacy, it is prolonged and often retarded by misinformation and the absence of comforting agreement or empathy from peers wrestling with the same confusing and frightening process of discovery. Boys who feel free enough and trusting enough of each other to share their fears and confusion often pass through a stage of sex play that, for the cooperation, alleviates some of the more exaggerated fears (beginning with "Oh, my God! What is happening to me?") much faster. Finally, heterosexual boys whose culture openly encourages heterosexual experimentation will skip this pseudo-homosexual stage altogether and experiment instead with experimenting girls.

Sex Play

Sex play among the middle group of boys in transition is bound to be homosexual in appearance because it is sex play and because there are no girls around. Separating the activity from any moral judgment, the experiments have the effect of testing the equipment among the ranks before venturing into the field wherein you intend to use it for serious purpose. The reason male youngsters can participate in gay sex but not define it as homosexual is partly because some do not know the labels well enough yet, and have not been schooled in sexuality at all, properly or otherwise, and partly because the closest they feel to a genuine emotion is merely curiosity. Peers suggest arbitrarily that certain forms of behavior at certain ages are okay, while others are not, and the rules depend on where you grew to pubescence, and when, and with whom. Experimental oral stimulation might be all right for one gathering of apprentice adolescents, while kissing, for example, likely would be taboo for most. That distinction is precisely the sort that immediately begins to separate straight and gay boys, especially in the minds of the gay ones. For him, kissing would be one of the most significant signs of his sexuality, as it would for a heterosexual boy during his initial experiences with a heterosexual girl.

Among boys, the straight boy would be comfortable with group or even mutual masturbation, but kissing might stretch even his undefined boundaries and make him uncertain and uneasy.

Most boys seem to be masturbating even before puberty, though some learn later, and many learn with, or from, a friend. The more adventurous among them also participate in genital sucking and anal intercourse, especially openly gay boys, who seem more likely than their heterosexual counterparts to admit that during this period they demand further exploration and excitement. The sex play feels good. It is fun, and rarely is there any indication, at least among those unaffected by orthodoxy, that they believe the activities to be terribly wrong, or any more wrong than merely naughty. They determine that despite their unspoken certainty that they are misbehaving in some way, they know also that sex play is not harmful, not unhealthy, and not dangerous. It seems almost perfectly natural, just another game. Truly pejorative words for it emerge only after the boys learn that adults have strong feelings about how the body should and should not be used.

In some childhoods, sex play is a training ground for later love games and provides valuable lessons for practical use in situations played out in later life. One of the characteristics of boyhood sex at this stage is that there tends to be no active or passive roles by permanent definition. Boys don't yet think of sex play as masculine or feminine, nor do they know the gender rules and distinctions. They seem just to try whatever they can think of.

For a gay boy, however, an added dimension hovers over every incident of sex play. The gay boy feels a vague sense of a desire for closeness during these exploratory sessions. He may be more aware of how much he admires the person with whom he is playing, or he may long for some communication that the sex play suggests more meaning to the friendship, maybe not even knowing why; whereas the straight boy's plain and simple goal is to experience whatever new physical pleasure becomes available, including, eventually, the stunning physiological experience of orgasm.

Boys experiencing their first orgasms seldom know what it is, and in some cases it scares the hell out of them, and then, of course, draws them right back to whatever activity made the orgasm happen. Oddly, it is the experience of orgasm that in many cases heralds the beginning of the decline of innocent sex play. Orgasm is sufficiently powerful a pleasure as to inspire reflection and meditation and, depending on any number of factors, the participants' activities may increase or decrease at this—pardon the expression—climactic stage of pubescence. If a boy is comfortable among his peers, even if he is gay, he generally will continue the experimentation with other boys.

The gay boy who already is internalizing the homophobic messages and who already feels distant from his peers probably will retreat into fantasy. The straight boy does not feel the same pain as the young gay, who not only wants sexual release and experience but affection and solace as well.

Also, boys who are concerned about parental approval and who will not do what they imagine their parents would not approve of, now will reject as bad, sinful, dishonorable, or disobedient their own behavior and even the feelings that led to their behavior. Orgasms shake foundations.

If the gay child feels responsible in any way for his parents' suffering, or even if he only feels mildly guilty for being, however passively, however blamelessly, the subject of such a debate, where does he go for solace? For reassurance? For even the pretense of understanding? Where does he go? One youth approached his twenty-eight-year-old brother and suggested that he might be bisexual, using bisexuality as a hopefully less damnable device. The brother advised him against bisexuality because of the possibility of AIDS. They never talked about his sexuality again.

The gay boy does not even belong to a family on whose collective shoulder he can lean. He cannot naturally rely on the protective context of "us" and "them." In most cases, the "we" in the family lexicon does not include that family's gay child without at least some exceptions. Even among his siblings there are competing expressions of protectiveness and rejection, as a brother or sister defends his or her gay sibling's right to be who he is while simultaneously wondering why he can't be like everybody else.

In the cruelest of circumstances, the family excludes him entirely—banishes him, declares him literally nonexistent and/or dead. The message is clear in fact to nearly all of them that they can be expelled in one way or another from the family for being gay. Nobody else in the gay's experience knows so graphically or with such certainty that he actually can be kicked out of his family. Bullies, burglars, robbers, killers, junkies, pimps, and whores are less likely to be expelled for being who they are. Most gays, adolescents especially, who are aware that they are gay also are aware that they could be exiled from their families merely for being gay.

If the gay child feels any sense of unconditional membership at all, he probably feels it toward an entity outside the family: to the minority, however hated by his family, of the people he encounters who are similarly different. If he does not encounter them, or if the gay chronological peers whom he does encounter already have been so terrified or traumatized by their own family's opposition to homosexuality that they dare not reveal themselves to him, the gay child remains adrift in ignorance, about himself, about the existence of people like him and the fact that they have a history, about almost anything upon which he could momentarily lean his flagging sense of self-worth.

The dearth and/or the suppression of information, let alone positive information about gays, keeps gays from learning about themselves and from knowing about their counterparts in the community and in surrounding communities. Typically, Hollywood presents the gay man as one of two extremes, a frivolous fop, as in a hundred films, or a homicidal maniac, as in *Silence of the Lambs*. The most sympathetic portrayals, such as the character played by George Carlin in Barbra Streisand's *Prince of Tides*, still is that of a tragically lonely and sad misfit. Despite the heroism of politicized gays in the past decade, and despite the positive, courageous, and sensible responses by much of the population, gays still are invisible in most communities. Historically, such information as the young gay man might get about homosexuality either is untrue or is so negatively punctuated or so poisoned by derision, it only nurtures rather than dispels the gay recipient's self-condemnations.

Like a chemical reaction, numerical superiority blended with ignorant fear turns into hostility and disdain; numerical inferiority mixed with the fear of disdain turns into some degree of shame. Distinct behavior simply emerges from there. For their self-protection and security, the majority heterosexuals declare themselves righteously superior and begin the process of rationalizing ostracism; for his defense, the lonely minority, puzzled over such control as he does not seem to have over his predicament, finds a way to embrace, employ or live with his humiliation. In rarer instances he rebels against it. More commonly he hides from it in a variety of self-altering ways.

Less support and more opposition is his lot. The extra forces fighting against him coupled with the support he does not get result in a daily one-two punch combination that borders on the ridiculous. Think of it: added to the passive-negative realities of a paucity of positive information and an absence of like-minded supporters is an avalanche of negative information, ridicule, and condemnation, most aggressively and destructively heaped on the individual from the hallowed hypocrisy of organized religion. Of all ironies in his life, the flat-out winner is that the institutionalized center of comfort, encouragement, solace, hope, and love for the oppressed sub-communities of the globe is the gay boy's most unrelenting and insidious organized tormentor. A man born gay faces constant messages of condemnation to eternal damnation from ancient organizations that paradoxically profess to hold all creatures of the deity to have been created in his image and to be objects of his affection and love.

In their most dazzlingly generous protestations of concern, representatives of organized religion have been viciously back-handed in their offerings of welcome and assistance to the gay population. A benign and sympathetic cleric of the Catholic Church, whose gay biological brother had been diagnosed as HIV-positive, recently told a television audience that the Church finally was coming around to accepting homosexuals for being who they are, created as they were by the same God, but that it merely rejected—and asked that they reject as well—"acting on" their homosexuality. So those gay youths in the TV audience who might have been hoping for a kind word from a sympathetic churchman were to understand that the Church no longer condemned their existence, only the manner in which they might most naturally express their affection, support, and love for one another.

A common prayer among gays who still believe in the device is the prayer that God will realize His mistake, refer back to the original design and repair the gay child, make him right again, correct the error, change him back. Gay adolescents trying not to be gay pray desperately, saying, "Please, God, I'll do anything, please make me straight."

No person—even if fervently supported, encouraged and goaded by his family and friends—can escape so constant and undefended a barrage of criticism, ostracism, and condemnation without eventually applying some of the negative judgments and evaluations to himself. This internalization of some percentage of the abundant negative messages about himself for his different-ness, especially in the absence of any information in support of himself, takes root, nurtures itself, takes further nourishment from the society at large, and ultimately becomes the growing gay man's most relentless, insidious, and treacherous enemy. To one degree or another, every gay youngster in our society comes equipped with a powerful coefficient of self-loathing.

Adaptive Strategies

The internalization of those negative judgments and values, beliefs and attitudes, in the young gay man most often leads to a
feeling of and becomes equated with inferiority and inadequacy,
which eventually converts into shame and embarrassment. From
that the gay man erects a series of defense mechanisms and
behavioral alterations—adaptive strategies—that help him cope
with the shame. He relies heavily on two variations of secrecy
and concealment, suggest Vivienne Cass and Betty Berzon. In
the one variation, a herculean form of denial, he conceals as
much from himself as from the dominant world; in the other he
is much more duplicitous and, paradoxically, somewhat stronger
for it. The mechanism of denial includes, as it did in my case,
a convenient form of memory erasure that maintains the denial
by concealing from the conscious mind any record of an incident,
feeling, scene, or fact that would challenge it. Many gay young
men also strive consciously and subconsciously to deny even the
different-ness that they found so undeniable in childhood, and
later deny themselves more aggressively by effectively numbing
themselves to their own feelings of attraction to another member
of the same sex, which attraction all the while feels perfectly
natural, so that they are consciously fighting to deny and suppress their own nature. Generally, gays determined to hide from
themselves will try to bury or destroy whatever is real and build
instead a "straight and narrow" life, as I did, in an attempt to
deny membership in the minority and identify with and join the
majority. Some gays even stretch this to behaving antagonisti-
cally or aggressively toward gays, as did lawyer Roy Cohn or the
late FBI founder J. Edgar Hoover, long believed to be gay and
long known to behave as if he despised gays—both eminently
possible and not at all mutually exclusive.

Other gays, who work face to face against some of the
spasms of shame and who manage to summon the courage to
defy others, live a more boldface, outwardly directed lie, aimed
year after year at deceiving the dominant society into believing

they are card-carrying members, while secretly lurking in the traditionally shadowy world of gay nightlife and the fluctuating security of a semi-secret gay fraternity. They hone their skills as youngsters and teens, and urban centers seem to be the spawning ground for the cleverest, the toughest, and the most sophisticated of these deceivers. The more intentionally secretive gay works against his shame, perfecting, if he can, a multiple identity, and living at least a dual life, perhaps one more complex even than that, trying to confirm a role expectation on the one hand and satisfy his acknowledged needs on the other. He may begin as a pre-adolescent, with a hidden life of masturbation and secret sexual fantasies, not denying himself but creating a hidden closet for his true self and a masquerade for the larger, more hostile world. He may develop then a sharper wit or a broader knowledge of current trends in order to stay on top, gain approval or acceptance in his society, and make the differences between him and his peers less conspicuous or perhaps counterbalanced by his more competitively formidable presence. He may also be fragmenting parts of himself in a way that prevents him from being intimate, for fear of discovery or disclosure and the unspeakable condemnation and abandonment that would result.

Teenagers from the New York City school system who said they knew that they were gay from as early as six, seven, and eight years old said they concealed it from their families for fear they would be beaten for it or kicked out of the house. In some instances they risked revealing themselves to favored aunts or trusted older siblings, who merely confirmed the dangers of revealing the information to anyone else. The most confident among them said that he would not tell his mother that he was gay until he was out of her house and economically independent from her; even then, he said, he might not tell her because it would only hurt her. He was sure it would not inspire any new sympathy or affection for him.

Their heterosexual peers on the street knew these boys were gay, but the codes of their streets were primitively simple, requiring only that they be able to defend themselves if and when attacked for being faggots. (Gay life should be so uncomplicated everywhere.) One fragile, diminutive, effeminate boy, a dance student born in the Dominican Republic who bragged that from early childhood he always liked to act flamboyantly in public, though he tried to avoid it in front of his mother and siblings, said he evaded periodic beatings by becoming something of a comic in a threatening crisis. Without feeling that he might be humiliating himself but was instead "getting over" on or outwitting his tormentors, he would perform his way out of a beating, mimicking and making fun of himself or famous pop stars, particularly the more androgynous such as Prince or Michael Jackson. Gays who are naturally predisposed—as some are in every culture on the globe—toward effeminacy will make efforts to reject such effeminacy as they are inclined to display, subdue it and create in its stead a "straight" persona.

Another gay dance student, a broad-shouldered six-foot-three fifteen-year-old from Antigua, also effeminate but less exaggerated about it, told how he had to fight somebody in his South Bronx neighborhood once or twice a week on the way home from school, until he became tough enough to have developed a ratio of wins that evidently took the fun out of jumping him. "They left me alone after I beat them up a couple of times," he said matter-of-factly.

Two other ways of handling the inescapable shame of being different are through isolation and its diametric opposite, confrontation, and even the isolation takes separate forms for separate reasons. The gay man isolates himself not only for his differentness but for fear of detection, lest his difference become known. He is both afraid of himself and of other people's fear of him, afraid of social isolation. Often, the motivations for concealment blend, so he isn't sure what he is afraid of or why he is hiding.

The gay child or pre-adolescent who chooses isolation as his primary strategy simply will socially and even emotionally separate himself from both the family and the peer group and withdraw into a more severely internalized world. His detractors tend to suspect that he is gay, but rather than outwardly berate

him for it, they will berate him for his more obvious transgres-
sions, rejecting them. They may still even use the word *faggot*
in describing him, but it will be a reference to the first, colloquial
definition of the word, popularized in the late 1950s and closer
in meaning to *nerd* or *dweeb*.

The confrontational personality handles his shame through
exaggerated flights into femininity and flamboyance, flaunting,
taunting, posturing, wearing his different-ness as a badge, "flam-
ing" as if to challenge the entire critical society by rejecting its
rules and codes, paragraph for paragraph, saying, "Is this what
you mean by the names you call me? Is this what you say I am?
Well, then, watch me!"

Lee, the fifteen-year-old New Yorker who described himself
as a bisexual on the way to admitting he was a homosexual,
remembers distinctly adopting this confrontational way of facing
the pressure from the street. "I always wore my hair long," he
said, "and I would react fast to whatever people told me about
myself. Like, 'You say I'm gay? Okay, fuck you, I'll be gay. Here,
watch this!' I scared myself, though. For a while I had a lot of
sex with a lot of females just to prove a point."

Probably every gay person goes through one of these alter-
natives, and most go through all of them in varying degrees and
speeds. Managing the crisis of being different and surviving the
period requires and fosters a heroism and a level of creativity
not demanded of the average young person, to say the least. It
also can inspire an almost warrior-like ferocity, which ultimately
is required to combat the seemingly endless criticism and ostracism heaped upon the gay youth and helps people overcome
those barriers so they can begin the process of self-acceptance.

Eventually the gay youth gains independence from the by-
products of being different and thus isolated. He becomes more
creative and aware for having to constantly ask himself who he
is in relation to what he sees around him, as well as for having
to monitor himself in order to evade detection or derision from
his family and his peers. He acquires a heightened compassion
and sensitivity from his constant identification with fellow vic-

tims of cruelty. He eventually will accumulate an encyclopedia of strategies for adapting to and overcoming a puzzlingly hostile environment. This can evolve over decades, through personal crises or some cataclysmic catharsis. Those who do break through are permitted entry and encouraged to peek, tiptoe, burst, explode or leap into the next, terrifying stage of their development, the whole process of self-acknowledgment.

Self-Acknowledgment

Thinking the Unthinkable

Well into the project of writing this book—in fact, while
thinking about the intended content of this chapter and the
transition from *acknowledgment* of homosexuality to actually
coming out, I was offered the weekend use of a friend's
country house north of Rhinebeck, New York, and a car to get
there.

Driving through the Catskills triggered a series of feelings,
then memories, then remembered feelings, then more memories.
The process was subtle and as paradoxically unsettling as it was
soothing. It reminded me, as I struggled with my outline of the
gay man's psychological journey, that I still am on my own jour-

ney, ever rounding unexpected corners and encountering unforeseen detours.

I involuntarily recalled that for many of the summers of my early life, my family rented a summer cottage in the Rockaways, as did other native New Yorkers in the years before air conditioning became available to everyone of our economic class. We took a cottage near the beach and the year-round home of my mother's closest sister.

I remember those summers with a great and wistful fondness because I spent a good deal of that time with my cousins, one exactly my age and the other close enough to be a playmate. The last summer we spent there was the summer of my mother's pregnancy with my sister, and therefore the last summer I would have my mother's full attention, or even some of it, by my admittedly singular prejudices. I must have been eight years old because my sister was born when I was nine.

My mother had not yet suffered the heart attack she would have at the age of forty, and I remember that summer as one of the last that she was healthy and that we were close. We would spend our days frolicking on the beach and our evenings walking the boardwalk. My mother had a really strong throwing arm and a fondness for playing boardwalk games. She was a champ at knocking over stuffed penguins and overfringed Raggedy Andy dolls lined up as deceptively easy targets.

After that summer we moved to Long Island and traveled every day to the beach club at Lido Beach, except for one August when I was in junior high school. My parents decided to break tradition and vacation in the Catskills for an entire month. Moreover—and this was very unusual, because we did not have a particularly strong identification with a Jewish world—we stayed at the Brickman Hotel, and in all the intervening years I did not recall that fact, let alone the following events, until the spring of 1993 and the ride north on the New York State Thruway.

At the Brickman, we occupied one of a string of small cottages, though we had one of the larger ones. My mother and sisters and I lived there for the month; my father came up on weekends.

Within a day or two, I now recall, I spied a lifeguard at the pool, a very handsome young man, six feet tall with a lean, well-defined body, dark hair, and darkly tanned skin. I remember that as the summer wore on, I developed what I now would identify as a crush on the lifeguard and fantasized daily about just being close to him, imagining our sharing some undefined kind of affection. I behaved accordingly, I suppose, lingering too obviously around the pool, after the fashion of a stricken schoolgirl, and spending more time than I should have in the sun and in the water, even on cooler days. I seized every opportunity I could to talk to the lifeguard and tell him about myself. He seemed to take a special interest in me. He was particularly tender and gentle, unlike most of the men I had come across in my life, and his tolerance of what I now view as my pre-adolescent infatuation was astoundingly kind and patient.

In the last week of the vacation, on a rainy day, I found myself wandering about the hotel. The pool was closed. It was one of those aimless days when, because we had been there long enough to have explored every passageway and concocted every possible adventure, now there were no longer any new discoveries to be made. During my meandering I poked my head here and there and at one point even into the empty dining room, where I saw to my delight and surprise the lifeguard, working indoors for the afternoon, helping out setting up tables for dinner. He noticed me sticking my head in the doorway and gave me a warm wave. I waved back and then closed the giant door and sort of hung out in the lobby, not too far from the dining area, just to be near where he was working. Shortly after he finished his dining room duties, he wandered out into the lobby and sat down next to me. We chatted. He said something about the weather and it being a kind of indoor day but a boring one, and he suggested that we play a game of cards. I said I thought it was a great idea, and he turned up his enthusiasm, saying, "Come on, let's go back to my room."

I followed him back to the old part of the hotel, to a tiny staff employee room, very simple, with a bed and very little else. He sat down and pulled out a pack of cards and signaled for me to sit. We started to play cards and talk and laugh. I felt privileged, so wonderfully privileged that he would share his private time this way with me, especially in this little room that somehow felt so exotic and intimate, with such personal belongings as he had around him, and with the door closed.

Soon he reached out and began to play with my hair, in a teasing, tickling way at first. At least I think that's how it started. I responded, as I remember, first by laughing and then by tilting my head and closing my eyes, as if to suggest I was feeling great pleasure at the attention, which I was. Gradually the gestures developed into an affectionately romantic embrace on his part, and my quietly and naturally curling up and leaning into his big body, becoming wrapped in his arms, while he stroked my face and hair and kissed my forehead with precisely the kind of tender affection a heterosexual person might expect an older young man, say, a youth of seventeen or eighteen, to show a smitten girl of, say, thirteen or fourteen. He stroked my arms and touched my body with the most palpable tenderness and affection, and although I did not know quite what was happening, I knew it was exactly what I had wanted to happen, what I had hoped and had hopelessly daydreamed would happen.

The session in the lifeguard's room lasted a fair amount of time and then ended gradually, with very little said between us. In my memory, the lifeguard understood who I was and what I was, and he understood what I seemed to need at that moment. Remarkably, he did not take it too far. Like the imagined ideal, kindly heterosexual young man caressing the infatuated teenage girl, he did not go beyond what I needed or what he felt I could handle. He was not taking pleasure; he was giving. He was not lascivious, merely generous, in fact, loving. The episode ended without becoming any more complicated than tender fondling and the equivalent of a benign, soothing kind of petting.

I left the room and wandered around the hotel in an exalted

daze, absorbing the aroma of the place, the textures and sounds, the breadth of the rooms and the echoes of my time there, feeling amazed, exhilarated, and powerful for however long I permitted myself to feel it, before I applied my incredible trick of forgetting.

I am assuming that this happened after my school year with the neighborhood boy teaching me the arts of basketball and showering, because that adventure was sex play and this was something else entirely. A heterosexual boy could have become involved in the showering and the masturbating; this was something a heterosexual boy would never feel and never want. This was affection from a loving man, a connection between sensuality, sexuality, and emotion to a degree that my body, my senses, and even my emotions were acknowledging a reality that my mind, miraculously, soon would deny for nearly thirty more years.

It was a taste of what I now am calling acknowledgment. I suspect I was beginning to know quite well what the word *homosexual* meant, although what never ceases to amaze me is the immediate subsequent memory erasure. Evidently, as soon as I received information that brought me closer to understanding my natural self, I did something destructive with the information. I buried it somehow.

This boy that I was, for those moments at the Brickman Hotel, now knew what he was and who he was, and for a blissful series of peaceful, loving, otherwise unforgettable moments, he accepted it and accepted himself. Then, within hours, days, or weeks—I honestly don't know how fast; I only know for how incredibly long—he forgot it entirely, probably simultaneously cherishing the memory and holding it in contempt, until contempt won control of his conscious memory. He must have found it unbearable until years later, when he tripped over it while plodding along on a journey of self-reclamation and discovery, as part of the elongated and characteristically interrupted process of developing his identity as a gay man.

This stage in which an individual acknowledges the nature of his different-ness begins with making the first connection between the already recognized different-ness and the added recognition that the difference is same-gender attraction. My first perfunctory glimpse of myself in this light may have been at six years old in the locker room of the Fresh Meadows pool, but I was too young to understand and too unconditioned to recoil in horror. My first conscious visitation to this stage, as far as I now know, happened at the Brickman Hotel.

The maturation of my acknowledgment, such that it freed me to think about entering the next level, *coming out*, occurred as I was nearing forty and suffering alone with myself and my flu for days. In the interim I managed to evade acknowledging my true self and to deny the existence of any indicating evidence or supporting fact or feeling. In a better world, my acknowledgment might have occurred over a definable, linear time frame beginning and ending during my adolescence rather than at random, forgotten intervals, exploding and then disappearing mysteriously throughout the first four decades of my life. As I reflect on the process, even while vivid new memories of seminal chapters of my autobiography burst into my consciousness, I am reminded of the even greater mysteries of multiple personality disorder, whose sufferers create whole, distinct personalities and compartmentalize them in response to unimaginable duress. Following the repression of memories of rejection experiences so painful as to be unendurable, the mind invents separate, new characters to share the unspeakable damage.

The heroism of the human spirit, both voluntary and involuntary, truly is amazing, and nearly indomitable, so often reshaping experiences of rejection, ostracism, and deprivation into occasions for unprecedented creativity and adaptation. While as exaggerated a response to horror as multiple personality disorder clearly is dangerous to the integrity of the individual, there is no mistaking that it is as intensely creative a maneuver as humans are documented to have invented. In a less complex and less profound way, but borne of the same kind of wondrously creative response mechanisms, gay personalities reinvent themselves too.

First Romance

In the last chapter I spoke about having the feeling of different-
ness before having any word to describe it. "Why do I feel
different? What if anything is wrong with me?" Now I am talking
about making the connection and beginning to ask the question,
"Well, then, who am I?"

The acknowledgment stage couples sexuality with affection,
admiration, and infatuation, falling, for all practical purposes, for
another boy or man. When the memory mechanisms of a man
permit him to enjoy the reverie about his experiences in this
stage, whenever he experienced it, the dominant feeling about
the memory is its purity, its self-effacing, self-offering, and self-
less innocence. It is analogous to first love, pure and simple,
though for a gay man it could happen to him at any point along
his periodically aborted chronology. Whenever it does, he will
likely say that he remembers no period in his life as absolutely
pure and as guileless as this one.

That, of course, is when it all goes well.

At a distinct advantage are those gay boys fortunate enough
to have this experience at the age heterosexual boys are experiencing its counterpart. They eventually accept their homosexuality much more easily than gays who manage to frustrate and
delay the experience. More commonly, unfortunately, men rediscover belatedly their same-gender romantic inclinations who
have repressed their sexuality for years, or whose adaptations
because of shame or guilt have smothered or prohibited them
from enjoying their natural sexuality. The initial experiences,
however, will feel the same.

But for others, these young affairs seem to have an emotional and sexual intensity for only one of the parties. A gay boy
will invest his emotions in the boy with whom he may be having
sexual relations. The gay boy wants the relations to continue, for
the relationship to grow and develop in an increasingly mature
and intimate way. The friend, often straight, is merely dabbling
in an exploratory stage of his own. The straight boy will decide,

determine, or discover, if he was not sure of it to begin with, that he cannot relate sexually to a male. He offers no return on the emotional investment. These affairs usually are terminated abruptly, either because one party fears being labeled as homosexual or simply because of some interference, like the threat of discovery. But because the gay boy is attached emotionally in a way that the straight boy is not, the gay boy learns, solo, some powerful early lessons about emotional love and rejection. Also, he is more likely to feel that something is wrong with him, that some flaw in his character caused the rejection by the otherwise loving friend. The rare gay boy possessed of an already solid sense of self-worth also could make the same discovery in reverse, concluding that the profound change he felt emerging in the relationship from, say, sex play to love play had affected only him, in which case he may reject the straight sex partner for the lack of a more meaningful reciprocity. Either way, he is the only one who feels loss.

Gay boys frequently look for older men to show them what being gay is about, or to be initiated into gay sex, and that initiation is for many a necessary part of the transition from childhood into adulthood. Some look for an adult who will reassure them that their feelings are acceptable. Comfort and reassurance are of monumental significance at this point. The boy trusts and learns from the man, offering his loyalty in return.

Both parties thus risk possible exploitation, as does anyone in a relationship that relies heavily on trust and loyalty. All variations of cases of undeniable sexual exploitation exist, of course, and with partners on both sides of the gay and straight divide. But being exploited does not inhibit homosexuality any more than it does heterosexuality; the gay does not turn away from homosexuality because of the exploitation. He may develop, as any spurned lover, an attitude of distrust, and he may generalize it to all men. He may also add the betrayal to the arsenal of rationalizations for his sexual inhibitions or his repressed sexuality, but it will not change him into a heterosexual.

It seems to be a not uncommon rite of passage, and the

following story of passage through adolescence into homosexual adulthood contains these elements as well. Andy, who has been openly gay for all of his adult life, beginning with late adolescence, tells of being sexually "exploited" at pubescence by an older boy who went on to grow up heterosexual, which Andy now firmly believes he was all along. In retrospect, the slender, athletic Andy also believes that the exploitation was mutual, and in fact amounted to a comfortable, relatively blameless way for him to find out and even verify what he already had suspected was the difference between him and others he knew.

"It was the first long-term affair I ever had with a guy," recalled Andy, now thirty-seven. "But he was straight. He was about seventeen, and we were friends: he and his little brother, and I and my older brother. They lived on the street behind us, about two doors down in suburban Kansas City. We were sort of fringe families. My father was a clerk, the son of a sharecropper, and we never had a lot of money.

"This boy, Roger, had a really macho image, but when we would stay overnight at their house, I used to sleep with him, and my older brother used to sleep with his brother, David. When I was about fourteen, and we were sleeping at night, he started fondling me and taking my hand to fondle him. There was no emotional contact. At first he may have thought that I was sleeping. I did pretend that I was, and I think that was important for him in the beginning, because there was sure to be no emotional transaction for him that way. I was excited, I was titillated, and I think it was the first sex that I had when I was sexually mature."

Aware by that time that he was attracted to men, and having had experienced some sex play with men before, Andy says he felt at this encounter that Roger was exploiting him, but mainly because he knew Roger was more attracted to women.

"It developed from fondling to oral sex and, finally, anal sex," recalls Andy. "I was always in the passive position. There was no kissing, although I remember that I wanted that. For me, it was a romantic situation, at least in my mind. Here was someone older and, I thought, very sexy. I felt he was using me just to, you know, get his jollies, but at the same time his desire still really excited me. So maybe we were using each other. I also felt very conscious of being, like, awakened.

"It's really strange, while you're doing this, there's something that makes you forget it the next day, or that keeps repeating inside your head: 'I'm not really like that. I'm just having fun.' And then you go about your life as if you are not gay, though some part of you knows that you enjoyed it too much. I said to myself, 'I could stop this any time.'

"At the same time, I had a little red-haired girlfriend. I used to try to feel her tits out of some kind of social responsibility, possibly partly living up to the macho ideal, you know, getting to feel tits and then talk about it after. I also really wanted to know if I could be attracted to this girl. What would this feel like? Would I enjoy it? I think also I wanted to know what was available. But I felt no desire, just an intellectual curiosity.

"In Kansas, most people did not go on to college. When you graduated high school, it basically became time for you to become a man. When I graduated, I had to confront who I was. I was involved in the community theater, and I had a couple of sexual experiences with people there. After I had sex with a man, I would feel terrible and pray that if I was forgiven, it would never happen again. I denied that I was gay as often as I confronted that I was gay. Whenever I was denying it, I always saw the events as one-time events that were never going to happen again. And then a month later, it would happen again, and I would pray some more. It was too taboo to even mention in confession. So I didn't confess it. Not ever."

Initially, according to men like Andy who can pinpoint the moment in their memories, the first instant when a man consciously perceives himself as a homosexual seems to him as if it is either a realization about another man, a person outside himself, or the acknowledgment that a dream or fantasy—or a nightmare—seems to be coming to life. He may not even be fully aware of what homosexuality is or what it means, but only aware of his same-gender attraction or desire as being the difference between him and other boys and as feeling like a natural part of himself.

Most gay men who have struggled through their development to the degree where they now are openly gay recall incidents in their youthful past that would support that the acknowledgment of sexuality first occurs between thirteen and eighteen (according to R. Troiden and E. Goode, in a 1980 article in the *Journal of Homosexuality*), just at the time in life as most heterosexuals. Many gays, I among them, apparently do not make the connection until well after adolescence, though I suspect that they probably do make it and then repress the memory of it, as I did, which suggests that the development of a gay personality might be naturally and chronologically linear if the homophobic society exerted less pressure against it.

Such evidence as exists of this repression is found only in men who have recovered their repressed memories, but those memories at least represent more evidentiary proof than does the traditionalist suggestion that the absence of the memory proves the presence of the repression.

In fact, it seems more logical to suspect that what we might call the individual's human nature—the same kind of involuntary systemic reactions to stimuli that make the rabbit run, the snake bite, and the heterosexual man's head snap when his gaze crosses that of a beautiful woman—kicks in sexually at about the same time for everybody and becomes recognizable at the time it kicks in; that boys, for instance, first acknowledge the nature, direction, and depth of sexual feelings when they first begin to experience them, whichever their sexuality.

The difference for homosexuals, especially in a homophobic world, is that many of them take one look at the feeling that has kicked in and immediately make every effort to kick it back out, so preprogrammed are they to revile anybody who seems to feel this way. They then may succeed to varying degrees in repressing these feelings for years, or even for life, using powerful psycho-intellectual devices, including denying that it could have happened or even completely forgetting that it did.

Thus, like all the stages of a homosexual man's development, *acknowledgment* may only appear to defy a traditionally definitive categorical description and a linear path, because the path has become so interrupted by the individual's periodic acquiescence to society's opposition to him. Developing gays enter the stage naturally and tear themselves away from it unnaturally, denying what they have experienced to be true and forgetting parts of their own developmental life until such time as they summon and employ whatever courage, frustration, agony, desperation, or strength they require to return again to the same stage and follow it through to some semblance of completion.

But how could it be otherwise in such a hostile society? The gay personality's acknowledgment might better parallel the linear development of a heterosexual personality's acknowledgment if it was accompanied by parallel support from the society, by comparable encouragement and acceptance, but it is not. In the best-case scenario in our homophobic world, an exceptional youth from an exceptional family may begin to experience his self-recognition at pubescence and follow through logically and naturally with subsequent experiences over a comfortable period of time, until he is sufficiently convinced of and satisfied with who he is to introduce himself that way to the outside world, however hostile it is.

Other gays, however, and arguably most others, play an incredible range of variations on that theme, all marvelously creative. The range includes varying degrees of developmental interruption up to and including developmental retardation and even circumventing stages entirely.

At the earliest, the emerging individual is consciously aware that the information he is receiving about his homosexuality is phenomenally relevant, but in the absence of positive information or the possibility of support for his true sexuality, he still prefers to think of himself as a heterosexual. For that bizarre and unnatural insistence he receives tremendous support from members of the dominant heterosexual community.

These first clear indications of homosexuality, then, are sure to become unwanted feelings and unacceptable to the preferred self-image. Instead of proceeding with the linear process of acknowledging his sexuality as does his heterosexual, chronological peer, the gay youth begins instead to develop strategies to evade the progress, or to block or postpone it, while he may involuntarily marshal what strengths he can to accept the possibility in the absence of support.

The gay youth in our society fluctuates constantly between acknowledging and denying himself. Most gay men's memories of that early period are extremely clouded. Often the experience is emotionally confused because one of the evasive, adaptive strategies for dealing with it is to confuse it.

Adaptive Strategies

The struggle that emerges from this stage is between the powerful drive the gay youth feels to be what he now has acknowledged to be his true self and the equally powerful desire to be almost anything but, to yield instead to the seemingly cosmic homophobia by trying to ignore, deny, or rid himself of what knowledge he has about who and what he is. By yielding to the pressure, however, he divides the self-image, continues to internalize the outside pressures, and continues to plummet toward "self-alienation," according to Vivienne Cass. Whether he concludes that his sexual feelings are natural or aberrant, he still is very likely to apply the conclusion to his whole self, to his character, not just to a part of himself that he calls his sexuality, or his libido, or his psychotic grandmother's tragic legacy. Whereas in the earlier stage he might have been convinced enough of the evil of mere difference to have evaluated his different behavior as wrong, now he is ready to regard his character as wrong and basically to assist the homophobic world by joining them in their blanket condemnation of him and his worth.

Rather than alienate the critical straight world in an almost retaliatory declaration of independence and defiance—which would indicate either colossal bravery or a pitiable inclination toward spiritual suicide—he may begin to alienate himself, especially if he has recognized his proclivities as gay and considers it an affliction undesirable to the degree that it is totally unacceptable, as many do. Whereas shame was his prevailing emotion at the earlier stage, guilt may become his prevailing motivational force in this stage, and he may proceed next with a conscious attempt at one or another form of denial, attempting to actively change himself, seeking a "cure" for his homosexuality through therapy or religion. He may bargain with his deity, offering acts of penitence in exchange for a conversion to heterosexuality. Many gay men freely recall the anguish of praying to and pleading with the God that created their feelings to re-create them differently.

He may in a more secular way, suggests Cass, disown responsibility for the feelings that identify his sexuality, claiming circumstantial influence to their origins or redefining the context in which his natural attraction most graphically manifested itself: he was drunk that one time; he was high on drugs that other time; he was taken advantage of in his adolescence; he was asleep when first lured.

Some gay men consciously suppress their homosexuality, knowing full well the extent of their gay-ness but refusing to "act on" their sexuality, as the clergy has called it, refusing to participate in a homosexual romance of any kind. They may intentionally limit their intake of information regarding homosexuality, saying to themselves, "It may be true, but I'm not going to do anything about it," or, as Andy remembers saying so many times: "It was a one-time event. Please forgive me, God, I'll never do it again."

Some really repress the information, which is a different tactic entirely, because it is not conscious. I fall headlong into this category, living a life that was acceptable to the dominant society but that was not at all authentic, until I had exhausted

every avenue of self-fulfillment and still was desperately unfulfilled. Many gay men do exactly the same, men who know they
are romantically interested in men but choose to be with women.
They marry, have children, even continue to love their spouses,
though more socially than romantically, and they live whole lives
as unfulfilled as the heterosexual man's life would be if he were
bound by some unimaginable pressure to live his life as a gay
man.

Other variations exist as well. Some gay men live lives ostensibly devoid of sexual feelings, as well as (or, in some cases,
instead of) in opposition to their own sexual feelings. They may
sacrifice their sexuality and live celibate lives, as the Catholic
Church requires of its clergy and recommends for gay men. In
some cases this path is the easiest for the gay Catholic to reconcile intellectually anyway, because he feels quite confident
that he can live comfortably without heterosexual activity, and
he accepts wholeheartedly that homosexuality is an aberration,
a sin against the laws of God that surely will earn him an eternal
sentence in hell. It does not disturb him that his sacrifice seems
senseless; his faith provides for a prayerful use for all personal
sacrifice as long as he continues to believe.

I had a patient who was an orthodox Jew. He found himself
in an arranged marriage, in which he could perform perfunctory
sex with his wife and be secure in the knowledge that perfunctory
sex was perfectly acceptable. Sexuality was so restricted in that
culture anyway, the institutionalized suppression helped maintain his unconscious repression, and it permitted the lack of
passion and the sense of disconnectedness he might have felt in
more natural, less orthodox circumstances.

Until one day, while he was traveling alone on a trip in
Israel, a young boy approached him. Suddenly the walls came
crumbling down.

In the absence of assistance from religion, nonbelievers may
simply re-create themselves as unaware of sexual needs of any
kind and appear as if they naturally were asexual. They seem to
just cut sex out of their lives—dangerously, I think, because

repressed sexuality may find its outlet in some equally powerful form of behavioral release that is far less socially acceptable than mere consensual homosexuality.

But the gay in denial, unable to see himself as "one of those people," may explore any number of strategies. According to Cass and Berzon, he may first rationalize his spasms of remembered homosexual interest as indicative of a stage he is or was passing through; he may explain it away with the help of what has come to be known as psychobabble, glibly suggesting that his father was not sufficiently active, or that his mother was overactive. He may compromise, claiming to be bisexual when he actually is not (most scientists distinguish bisexuality as a separate category altogether, according to the Opinion Research Corp. of Princeton) or claiming to be intellectually curious about the experience of homosexuality but fundamentally disinclined toward it. He may try desperately hard to fight it, straining while masturbating to think about making love to a woman; straining while making love to his wife not to think about what excites him most, the idea of making love to a man; or, most imaginatively, thinking about his wife making love to another man so that he can cloud the fact that what is exciting his interest is the man.

Very common, by the way, among gay men who have not acknowledged themselves and "come out" until after they have lived first as a married, "straight" male citizen, is the memory of powerful fantasies, not to mention real-life experiences, of their wives making love to other men while they watched. This is not to suggest that all couples who indulge in this kind of sexual voyeurism are circumventing one or the other's homosexuality, but many gay men who were previously married say that they used this device both to satisfy and mask their homosexual needs. Obviously, the wife who plays out the elements of this kind of fantasy is complicit in some basic way and probably is attracted for one reason or another to her husband's homosexuality.

Some men actively hate themselves for their homosexuality,

though they still indulge in homosexual liaisons, for which they hate themselves even more and hate their sexual partners as well. They keep their sexual contact free of emotional involvement, and some avoid repeated contact with any one partner. Others indulge in repeated sex with the same person but resent the person increasingly and treat him with contempt, which generally serves the self-hatred and guilty needs of both parties, each one feeling similarly embittered about his true nature.

Less frequently, men so threatened by their homosexual feelings will unconsciously evade the issue by converting their sexual or erotic attachments to inanimate objects, seemingly avoiding gender altogether. In rare instances of fetishism, they will find immediate or even long-term refuge in an erotic attachment to inanimate objects. During the run of this particular adaptive course, they never acknowledge or express the true nature of their sexuality, which is homosexual, because they are not aware of it. Not surprisingly, however, the inanimate objects that serve to arouse them often turn out to be the property of other men.

Sol, a forty-two-year-old New Zealander from a religious Jewish household, raised in an intensely sexually repressive community, describes now, as an adult, the fetishes that characterized his erotic life from prepubescence. A man of average height and weight who for the almost visible burden of his private shame appears more diminutive than he actually is, and who seems always to be trying to disappear tortoise-like into himself, Sol now understands his fetishes to be the probable means of his deferring his homosexual feelings. Nonetheless, he actually has decided to maintain the fetishes quite consciously as a permanent refuge from a sexuality that he perceives as damnable, fraught with the danger of violating the fabric of his entire religious and social training. He has so internalized his community's and his religion's condemnation of his homosexual nature that even now that he is fully aware of his involuntary adaptive strategy, he chooses to embrace it as a voluntary characteristic of his sad fate.

"I was not sexually attracted to any person during my childhood and youth," says Sol, "and all through my early twenties. I had sexual fetishes instead. I fantasized about objects like sneakers, eyeglasses, clothing. I felt aroused by them, which is what made me feel different from other kids. Most boys and girls seemed to be attracted to each other. I wasn't aware at the time that the objects that stimulated me were associated with a person, but I realized it much later: they all belonged to one household servant, a male. I hid that fact from myself somehow.

"At some point I became aware that mine weren't the right sexual feelings, or true sexual feelings, and I forced myself to try to have heterosexual arousal, but I never succeeded, not even toward my wife, who I married not out of sexual attraction but because it was a proper thing to do. Prior to getting married, I did question whether I would get aroused by a woman, and I even consulted with somebody. I said I was not attracted to women and asked if it would be wrong for me to get married. Would I eventually be aroused by my wife? The general consensus was that I should have no problem responding sexually, but I never did.

"At thirty-one, something changed. I was abroad in Jerusalem, in a park, when a young Arab in his late teens approached me. He propositioned me to go into the trees with him and have some fun. It was the first time that I got excited sexually. I had never pursued any sexual interests, no pornography or otherwise. Nothing. By this time I had been married seven years. It was 1983. The Arab boy and I held hands, sat and talked, and that was my first sexual contact for sure. I felt a tremendous amount of guilt. At the time I was considering relocating to Israel, and that whole experience unsettled me so much I didn't. Nothing like that had ever happened to me in New York. No one had ever approached me. About a year later, I forced myself to go to a male burlesque. At that time the fellows who danced would approach you for a private show and take you to a back room. I went. I didn't take off my clothes. I didn't expose myself, but I played with him sexually and got very excited. I didn't go back to the burlesque for another year, when I did meet another fellow and became friendly with him. I never had real sex with him, short of masturbation, or maybe oral sex, which is the extent of any of my sex, even to this point.

"Now I've more or less returned to some of my earlier fetishes to arouse myself. I feel at this stage that I'm permanently set back. I've sort of given up hope for any sexual or romantic connection. I feel that I reached a peak. I feel very unattractive to people, that the little bit that happened in my thirties was it for me."

Finally, another strategy for the self-denying gay is to develop an exaggerated moral antipathy toward gays, publicly condemning homosexuality with an impassioned fervor, even becoming an ardent gay basher. Again, this is not to suggest that all those whose teeth involuntarily clench at the mere conversational mention of homosexuals or who are driven to taunt, harass, beat, torture, shoot, or hang gays are themselves emotionally cowardly homosexuals. Just some. The rest are mere cowards.

Many men who know or suspect they are homosexual, or who acknowledge their homosexuality but find it anywhere from unacceptable to unbearable, employ variations of the strategy known clinically and colloquially as denial—whether through inhibition, suppression, or repression. These gay men on the run from their true selves risk powerful consequences, beginning with cutting off their true selves from their true feelings.

In the process of shutting down his erotic attraction over and over again for someone of the same sex, the gay in denial may be wearing down his natural spontaneity, eroding it in terms of sex, of affection, trust, devotion, even of affording himself the luxuries of surprise, delight, caprice, and whimsy. In the process of shutting down in this way, the gay man becomes emotionally restrained or detached. You cannot deny a fundamental aspect of your character without precipitating a chain of self-alienating reactions. The accumulation of a number of blunted sexual and emotional experiences over time sometimes blunts the emotional and sexual life as a whole. To counteract that, some men use drugs or alcohol to enhance the feeling of sexual arousal and thus inaugurate a whole new chain reaction of damaging consequences. These negative chain reactions are practically limitless.

Ironically, not all consequences of evasive adaptation are negative. Forced to live outside the male gender model because he cannot be defined by it, the gay who does not repress his homosexual nature in response to even self-alienation does become very introspective and deftly self-examining, beginning a process of self-discovery that ultimately becomes an integrated and then an integral part of a character strengthened by adversity. He pays much more attention than he might have otherwise to the grand shapes and sounds and to the minutest details of the world around him, conscious always of nuances and subtleties that would have passed him by were he not so assiduously careful, and for different reasons, about self-revelation and self-betrayal. The honed aesthetic sense attributed to gays is neither a fabricated nor an inaccurate stereotype, nor is it unearned. Like the great recipes of culinary history, it is an adaptation to impoverishment and oppression.

Increasingly, as society becomes more enlightened and the gay community becomes more cohesive, educated, and politicized, men are emerging who accept their homosexuality as natural, acceptable, even correct—or simply the hand they were dealt, as it were. These men seek more information in books and from therapy and experts, all in an attempt to actually face the question: Am I homosexual, and how can I best deal with that?

I may be flattering myself, but I think I might have felt an inclination toward that acceptance too in a way, but in those times the available information about gays was so negatively punctuated as to define me as a psychological cripple. I had not yet mustered the courage to stand in opposition to what seemed to be a world system. Homosexuality was a diagnostic category, an officially accepted mental illness. In the early 1960s, thinking for a short while that homosexual was what I was feeling, I sought information about it. Until recently such information was so laced with condemnation as to inspire even more self-alienation than if I had been left in ignorance. It drove me to retreat even further into repression. I do not think this would be true for me today. The cultural changes brought on just by the lifting in 1973 of the diagnostic category was staggering and has changed the entire picture immeasurably and irrevocably. The dissemination of better, truer, more positive information and the inexorable proliferation of its sources and resources would have provided me with the intellectual assistance and emotional support I required to make the necessary leaps, not to mention the encouragement the gay population in recent years has offered its members in the face of a common enemy even more powerful than the collective fears of the dominant population.

Because of this new information, the age of acknowledgment and then of coming out seems to be moving closer to their natural counterparts in the development of a heterosexual personality. That does not make the next stage any easier, only more timely, because now that he is beginning to confront himself and place his shame and guilt in a more reasonable perspective, the gay man is to confront an intensely unreasonable society, whose hostility toward him, incredibly, is far greater than his worst self-alienating condemnations could have prepared him for.

Of course, once we credibly establish that the prejudicially condemned gay youth converts the pain of his ostracism to a strength and creativity that ultimately benefits him, the question arises as to whether the more benign behavior of an increasingly enlightened dominant population would affect developing gays conversely, rendering them less independent and creative for society's embrace than they were under its condemning glare.

A theory we'd give worlds to test, it isn't worth losing any sleep over, at least for the balance of this century.

Self-Identification

Challenging the Definition of Homosexuality

I remember realizing what I was about to lose as I began to separate my already fulfilled but unfulfilling ambitions as a married, heterosexual father from my new ambitions for myself as a gay man. I first had to endure and survive a grieving period not only for the marriage and the life I had helped create, but for the blueprint itself and what satisfactions it never would offer me, never would have offered me, even if I had persisted in investing my faith and hopes in it.

Then I became much more attentive to the possibilities that were going to be mine as a gay man, most of which at this stage seemed to be negative, so preconditioned was I to viewing being homosexual as overwhelmingly negative. I remember saying almost aloud, whenever I observed gays or when I saw heterosexuals observing gays: "Is that going to be my life?" I asked myself. "Am I going to be that guy people look at in that weird way, then look around for someone to make that knowing kind of eye contact with? I see them look at each other as if to suggest that this stranger, who obviously is gay, is too strange, or funny, or creepy, or that he's something or someone to avoid. Am I going to be the stimulus for that? And will I know, every time, when people are viewing me that way and are communicating that way about me? And will it be better if I do know or if I don't?"

My preconditioned, homophobic prejudices rose too. Am I going to be like that old man, I thought, sitting at the corner in the Candlelight Lounge on Amsterdam Avenue, clearly alone and apparently despondent? Is that what's ahead for me? What about those guys in their forties, rustling in the brambles of Central Park, having anonymous sex? Am I going to know who they are now, those men high on cocaine I sometimes see going from club to club late at night? Are they my new community? Where will my intellectual companions be? Do gay men all talk only about fashion and style? Where do I fit in? Where are the gay couples? I don't see them. Are there gay men of substance?

In deciding to leave my marriage and honor my homosexuality, I had begun the process not only of identifying myself as gay, but of identifying myself as a member of a community with which I was absolutely unfamiliar, one opposed in form and sometimes substance to everything I had held dear. But I felt betrayed by everything I had held dear, having followed the prescribed blueprint to perfection and been rewarded by unremitting misery as a result. So I also felt that I had earned the right to be myself. Even in the confusion I knew that in order to return to some figurative crossroad in my life and follow this road not taken, I would be taking an uncharted journey into a culture and world where I would have no map, where I would not know the rules, and where I probably would have to surrender the rules that I did know, rules that had comforted me all of my life— rules that had steered me to the documented successes and security I had enjoyed despite my precarious sense of stability.

I did actually imagine that many of the familiar routes would be shut to me, and they were soon enough. The first casualty—thanks half to me—was my job. I was a department director of an institute for family therapy, now considering myself a gay man. Because I was breaking up my own family, I felt that I no longer could represent the family as an institution, a position I now consider to have grown in my garden of emotions somewhere between false humility and guilt-nurtured self-flagellation.

I also had incorporated the popular heterosexist notion that gay men could not have families and therefore could not be considered in favor of families or even part of any. I was a sheep in wolf's clothing, keeping a predator's eye out for vulnerabilities in me and my own kind.

Not surprisingly, the faculty and staff of the institute felt similarly, and they behaved accordingly. Rumors abounded about my relationship with John, and in my romantic—and perhaps self-destructive—delirium I was behaving so indiscreetly as to be verifying and then adding to the rumors daily. Although I had not publicly acknowledged my homosexuality, I had brought John to work a number of times. He was videotaping my lectures and my therapy sessions, and my affection for him no doubt was obvious to all.

Though never speaking directly on the issue of homosexuality or the possibility that I was a homosexual, the director of the institute made clear that he was becoming increasingly uncomfortable with me. It was not long before he announced a decision to change the structure of the administration. The board had combined my job with another. The majority of the faculty members under the authority of the holder of the new, combined position were women. So by implication it became increasingly clear that the position of department director of the newly combined department should go to a woman, and it soon did. I was thus removed from my position by the elimination of the position. In my own shame, and I suppose in the service of what I considered the higher priorities of the institute, I did not challenge the political manipulation of the hierarchy, nor did I actively recognize the prejudicial nature of the issue. I knew what was happening, but I already was so soaked in self-loathing, I felt I deserved it.

Almost willingly, and by my self-punishing vision, deservedly, I gave up my position professionally, and then I gave up my marital entitlement personally. I abandoned all the road maps, and I began to segue into a gay life I knew nothing about, with feelings of tremendous guilt and insecurity, and with John as my unlikely passport. John, who had lived on the edge all his life, who never had followed any of the established rules, who had lived in the world of the demimonde, partying at Studio 54, seemed in some way a guide who would help me navigate this mysterious, uncharted route.

As if to counterbalance my self-destructive, self-denying, defeatist behavior, I fought symbolic battles for my gay self. I lost them too. I can remember being on a lecture trip, checking into a hotel outside of Detroit with John. With great trepidation I specifically requested a double bed. When we got to the room, we found two single beds. It happened over and over again. The people at the desk would even say yes to the request for a double bed and then not provide it. I would go back downstairs and insist. John did not seem to care. To me it was a big issue, because each of our trips was one of my first trips as a gay man, and two battles were going on in my mind. I wanted to sleep with him, and I wanted it to be right to sleep with him. He had been down this road so many times before, he had no passion for the symbolism, and less for me, as it turned out. I meanwhile was met again and again with palpable scorn from such matrons as presided over the hotel desks.

That has never stopped happening, actually. It happens today. Years later, in Kyoto, Japan, I was traveling with my long-time partner on a dance tour with his company. We checked into a hotel, and we got single beds, despite my specific request. We returned to the desk, and the clerks behaved as if they did not speak English, so I motioned for a pencil and a pad and depicted two stick figures in a rectangle drawn on the plan of a double bed. As they watched, I defiantly added penises to the two stick figures. To my delight and surprise they said, "Yes, yes, yes!" and nodded enthusiastically. They then assigned us to a different room from the one we had seen. Jubilantly, triumphantly we marched to the new room and found two single beds. We covered the same ground three times. They simply refused to comply. We slept in two beds.

My family reacted to my life change almost the same way my institute had reacted, especially after they heard how my institute had reacted. Initially they simply distanced themselves from me. Conversations, calls, and letters became less frequent and more austere when they did take place. I tolerated that without objection, without asserting my right to their love and support. I think if I had pointed out to them that I still was their son and that I needed them more than ever, they might have come around sooner. Instead I played exactly the role I would have been expected to play, contrite and ashamed, and got exactly the results I might have expected to get, confusion and distance. We had enjoyed a close relationship, but I felt awful about what I was doing, ashamed about no longer following the traditional path they had expected. The final blow for them was my telling them that my job had been eliminated, and that although I could stay on as a faculty member and a clinician, I felt I no longer had a place there. I felt I needed to move on.

They were very wounded that I was dismantling my life, more so than they would have been if I was announcing merely a divorce. Then they would have worried about how frequently they might see their granddaughter and what would become of her. Now they worried if they would see their granddaughter and what she might become.

I was shedding everything that was familiar to them, and not only were they dealing with their own fears about my changing my life and breaking up the family, they also began immediately to cultivate new fears about homosexuality and AIDS. On top of that, they reacted not only with worry but with fear that they might be responsible for this aberration and, to the extent that they accepted the responsibility, they heaped guilt on themselves over their apparent failure as parents. My mother tried to get out of it by getting me out of it. She said repeatedly, "Are you sure you're doing the right thing? Maybe this is just a phase. How can you really be sure that you are gay?" as if I would dismantle my entire life on a whimsical suspicion.

My father simply stopped picking up the telephone as he always had to join in the conversation, to ask after the details of my life, or just to chat. I, of course, never would press to speak with him because I was so uncomfortable, feeling as if I had betrayed him even more than my mother, since we shared, after all, a common gender.

So, sigh, it goes. Just as the developing homosexual male begins to confront, endure, adapt to, and otherwise handle the reality that he is by nature and for all his life gay, just as he begins to invent strategies that punish and reward him for being different from most of his fellows, just as he begins to seek a way out of the involuntary hate-hate relationship he is nurturing with himself, the known world demonstrates that it despises him even more than he does himself.

The developing gay man often is his own worst enemy, but never is his only enemy. The cruel joke of this stage is similar to the comic adage: "Yes, you're paranoid, but, yes, everybody is out to get you too."

In the previous stage of development, the acknowledgment stage, the individual had to learn how to handle the self-alienation that emerged with the first signs of knowledge about his homosexuality. For me the process of getting to that point was jump-started suddenly when another boy called me a faggot, a public condemnation that drove me to enter (and then evade) a new level of self-examination and evaluation. Wrestling, however evasively, with the enemy within proved sufficiently distracting that I forgot, for a long, long time, that the other boy and thousands like him continued to exist and to exercise their virulent antipathy for persons different from them.

The problem never goes away, and the stage of development must be completed sooner or later. Whenever I confronted who and what I was, and what I thought of me, I would next have to deal with how others saw me, and why they saw me that way, and what if anything was I going to do about it?

Forgetting for the moment whether the manifestation of homophobia, mass hatred, mob rule or group-ist prejudicial behavior represents a pathology of its own, it still begets results. Persistent antagonistic behavior on the part of Group A tends to inspire personality alterations among members of Group B. When somebody calls you a faggot for the first time, your self-realization and self view becomes your number one problem. The person who called you a faggot becomes your number two problem, and maybe numbers two through two hundred unless you can invent ways to cope with the social alienation and cruelties of ostracism, prejudice, fear, and a hatred that by its very nature doesn't make any sense.

At this stage, having self-identified himself as a homosexual, the developing gay male must master three challenges. He must confront the accompanying recognition that other people define him as deviant; he must develop means for adjusting to the societal rejection in addition to adjusting to his own self-loathing; and finally, he must find a way to accept the resultant loss of the comfortable, safe, heterosexual blueprint.

On the one hand, the meaning of the category gay or homosexual has to change for him so he can include himself in it. But a cognitive change simultaneously must take place, wherein the gay man also can differentiate himself from society's image of homosexuals, because it has presented them as unacceptable and unworthy of inclusion in everyday life. The emerging gay man must summon whatever he requires to reject that hostile view and then find or create a view that is not so self-negating and ego-suicidal.

Naturally, he already has bought into the homophobic view, because to one degree or another he has been raised by homophobic people in a heterosexist society. At this point in his life he is more one of them than he is one of his own kind. Contact with the gay subculture usually provides him with the kind of information he needs about homosexuality to challenge the image he receives and has received from the straight world, and he may begin to see more acceptable possibilities for his future self in homosexual personalities whom he finds acceptable.

He then may begin, however early or late in life, to emulate such admirable or acceptable gay personalities as he encounters, or he may begin to create an acceptable personality of his own, based solely on what characteristics he independently deems acceptable to himself. Once again, because gays live outside the dominant society's rules, rewards, and allowances for what it considers acceptable behavior, no such rules and rewards exist for the behavior of gays. The range of possible adaptations of behavior are limited only by the imagination and level of courage, defiance, or terror of the participants.

Certain conditions intensify the emerging gay man's feeling of alienation. His change of self-identity to the point that he considers himself included in the category of homosexual is intimately related to the information about homosexuality available to him. The traditional silence on the topic clearly has hindered the development of most gay males, though now more positive information is circulating throughout the society, with more positive images, more possibilities for openness, and, eventually, a greater likelihood of tolerance. Indications that the development of a homosexual identity is occurring at an earlier age, though, probably mask the reality that increasing tolerance and openness are causing less retardation of such development, not any acceleration. The resistance is diminishing, but there still is no cultural assistance or encouragement for the growth of the gay personality.

But such indications do represent the shrinking of an overwhelmingly negative, isolated environment, making it less and less difficult for gay individuals to assist one another in their development, if only for their increasing visibility to each other. In many places in the country, they still are invisible.

This means that the accident of place of birth can become almost as crucial to the development of the personality as the accident of sexuality at birth. Homosexual children reared in urban centers, especially those where cultural diversity encourages or requires more tolerance, have a better chance at recognizing their commonality with other gay children, where statistics favor their presence. In more rural areas, however, even the concept of homosexuality as a statistical human reality may not be in a child's frame of reference. Alone without information or even a frame of reference for his thinking, a youngster can create a lot of fiction about who he is, and so can everybody else. He then may base his life on the story he tells himself with the help of the frightened and ignorant population surrounding him.

Paul, in his early twenties, a diminutive Mexican-American who moved recently to New York from a small town outside El Paso, Texas, remembers how hard it was to find any reinforcing commonality in his life and environs. "I hadn't had a lot of experience with men," he said. "I think a lot of it had to do with where I was living. El Paso is a big city, but you can't go anywhere without someone knowing you. A gay culture didn't exist. Down there the gay lifestyle is just not open. It's not visible. A lot of people who are gay go out of their way to hide it. I got my first taste of what passed for gay culture in the bars. We would drive down to El Paso and go to the bars. I went out with this girl who turned out to be a lesbian. We were covers for each other, though I don't think we consciously knew what we were doing at the time, or at first, anyway. Most people assumed that we were straight, and I think we thought we were straight at the time, or that we could be straight. We certainly were trying hard enough to be. Don't you find it interesting that we would find each other, though? I mean, eventually we were both saying to each other, like, 'Of all people!' We both were in denial or something.

"I didn't know there was a legitimate gay life out there. I had no frame of reference other than the bars. Even in the bars there were lesbians, gay men, straight kids, college kids. It was the late-night place in town. You could go there and be loose. It was a way to be a part of a subculture. No one made a point of being gay. They went out to the bar and then back into their closeted lives. When I did think about it, I felt even then that if I had to choose the gay lifestyle, it would mean I would be shunned by society. I imagined job discrimination, people being rude, not being able to have children. It's just not acceptable anywhere as a legitimate lifestyle. Or I didn't know that it was, or that it could be, at least until I went to New York. Then I realized that straight people could look at gay people and accept them as whole human beings."

Alan, twenty-six, says: "I was in my second year of high school in Kentucky. I found this magazine store. It's funny, I can't remember how I came across it, but it was such an important part of my high school years. It had these gay porno magazines. Oh, I do remember! My parents were having a party. I went with my mother to pick up the liquor, and when I turned around in this liquor store, I saw this magazine and said to myself, 'Oh, my God, this exists! There's this world!' We went home, and I drove right back out, got up my courage, and spent hours looking at those magazines. That began a pattern for two years in high school, when I would keep going back to this liquor store, always afraid I would be discovered, that they would call my mom. But that was gay life in Kentucky. That was all of it."

At this stage, having self-identified himself as gay, the developing individual slowly becomes aware of the real and imagined losses that he may suffer because of who he is. In particular, he must all but relinquish his heterosexual identity, and in the process give up the guidelines and expectations for a future as a successful heterosexual member of the community, including the respected roles of husband and father. But if marriage and family are not in his future, he wonders, then what is? What will give form and structure to his life?

Yael, nineteen, an aspiring actor raised in the Bronx in a religious family, attended Jewish schools and yeshivas and became a theater major at New York University. He spoke with a mixture of adolescent arrogance and childish fear about his pending struggles within his family with the consequences of what inevitably will be his life.

"On the way home from Passover dinner this past year," he began, "I stopped over at my brother's girlfriend's house. Her father is a despicable man, despicable. There was something on television about gays in the military when we got there. At that time I had no qualms about saying anything about myself, except to just come out and say, 'I'm gay.' I wasn't about to do that, just because I really didn't feel that was the way to handle it. Anyway, her father kept making comments about gays in the military. The first few times I ignored them. Then finally I just couldn't deal with it anymore."

Yael rose and began to reenact the parts in the conversations he recalled:

" 'Why are you saying these things?' " he asked the girlfriend's father.

" 'Because I wouldn't want to be in the military with gays,' " the man answered. " 'I don't want gays looking at me, pinching my ass.' "

"I told him, 'Don't flatter yourself.' I mean, how strange is this?" Yael said, this time addressing his audience. "In the heterosexual world, if someone is heterosexual, do you automatically think they're attracted to you? Yet when someone is gay, people think he's going to be attracted to every man. I think men who feel this way just don't want to be treated the same way they treat women, these macho, homophobic types. Anyway, I was rude to this man.

" 'These gay bars,' he said, 'they all meet people there just to have sex.'

"So I asked him, 'You ever been to one?'

"He said, 'No. Have you?'

" 'Maybe.'

"At this point my older brother started looking at me funny and said, 'Yael, are you dabbling? Or do you have friends who are gay? How many of your friends are gay?'

" 'I don't count. I don't sit there and say, he's gay; he's straight; he's gay.'

" 'Yael, if you're gay,' my brother said, 'I'll kill you.' "

Yael became momentarily solemn: "It was a stupid thing for him to say. This is the person, my brother, who is supposed to respect me.

"Then," Yael said, beginning to portray a small boy, "my middle brother asked, 'Yael, why did you want me to sponsor you for the AIDS walk? It benefits gay men. Why did you want me to sponsor gay men?'

"I started to cry," Yael said. "My brother seemed scared. I think he was genuinely frightened that I might be gay. He of course thinks it's unnatural, that gays are very unhappy and have many problems. Recently, my mom was asking me about another actor. 'Is he gay?' she said.

"I said, 'No.'

" 'Good,' she says, 'because he's an only child, and his mother isn't going to have any grandchildren if he is, and it's a very lonely life.' "

Yael sighed. "When I finally get to stop hiding," he said, "when I come out to my parents, I'm going to be so much happier, because when you're hiding something, it's a secret. And if it's a secret, it must be bad. And even though I can still tell myself I'm fine, that this is a gift, that I'm more sensitive, that I can look into other people's pain and I can look into myself, a gift in the sense that I have so many possibilities, so many ways to experience myself and change things, the fact is that I'm still hiding, and that means that I must still think there's something wrong with it. And, I guess, me."

At this stage, reports Vivienne Cass, letting go of the perception of himself as heterosexual plummets the developing gay into yet another profound loss, in fact, a series of losses.

Among them is the feeling both real and imagined of losses of present and future opportunities afforded heterosexuals. He may begin to imagine that pursuing a professional life will be prohibited—and, depending on his profession, it probably will be. He may not be allowed to teach children, serve in the military, or worship in the church he believed would welcome and comfort him. He must abdicate the right to be "good" in the eyes of God. He may then lose the loyalties of friends and members of his family or imagine these losses before giving them the chance to decide to abandon him. It doesn't matter which, except in degree, because both the reality and the appearance of reality erode his self-esteem. He has been programmed nearly from birth to suffer a tremendous loss of self-esteem at this juncture in his life, and he will lose it one way or the other. Either he will find his name on the cut list on the coach's bulletin board, or he will imagine seeing it there with such certainty that he'll decline the opportunity to look. He will either lose some of his legitimate places in society or imagine himself as having lost them. The feelings will be the same either way.

Some men so fear not being able to survive without the traditional blueprint or its traditional entitlements that they embrace an unwillingness to survive, a self-fulfilling prophetic desire not to survive, to succumb to the oppression and the will of the oppressor, as a way of accommodating to the world. That submission to helplessness will no doubt carry him into more severe depression. Almost every gay man will testify to a range of levels of this feeling of loss of a legitimate identity, from fleeting fantasies about the world faring without him to actual flirtations with the notion of suicide. This feeling of loss is a wound that must be mastered, though, in order for the developing gay man to move on.

Adaptive Strategies

Adaptations resemble one another at different stages, and an individual may employ the same strategy to combat the humiliation he feels from antagonism originating outside himself as he uses to combat his self-punitive insults. He might use a specific strategy in one stage for one reason, and a different one under different circumstances. People fighting rejection from both within and without often carry adaptive strategies from one un-expected crisis to another, like a sleeping bag or a Swiss Army knife, in case they need a tool to get them through whatever episodes of guilt, despondency, or humiliation they encounter, certain as they are that they will encounter them.

At this stage of development, however, the continuum of responses widens. In the face of continued shame and feared loss, some men retreat to internalize society's negative definitions of homosexuality, while others push forward to construct a def-inition that is positive and affirming. Those who internalize the antagonism infuse their personalities with the feelings of self-hatred and nourish their own lowered self-esteem. Others, who resist the dominant society's negative definitions of who and what they are, begin to respond to the challenges associated with this stage of development, evaluating the social condemnations more critically, replacing feelings of self-hatred and loss with in-creased self-acceptance and affirmation.

On one side of the response continuum, observes Cass, an individual resisting his world's condemnations may behave ex-uberantly about the notion of being different, celebrating that he is not fettered by the restrictions common to the average man, and privately and publicly diminishing the importance of het-erosexuality in his ambitions for achievement and fulfillment. This behavior may have its foundation in real feelings, and it may be an act, a dance choreographed to disguise real feelings, or it could be a combination of the two. It would function the same way anyhow. The individual finds being different—or acts like he finds it—special and exciting. He may be someone who from childhood has been developing the persona of a capricious nonconformist (precisely because subconsciously he may always have used nonconformity as an adaptive strategy for the antici-pated loss). He may never have known that the difference be-tween him and his friends was his sexuality, and now he may be relieved at his discovery, or his admission of the fact, espe-cially as he encounters more and more gay men who have gone through or are going through the same stage of development.

At the other end of the response spectrum, a very common strategy would be variations of my own: the person who in retrospect can point to milestones in his life that would indicate an acknowledgment of himself as homosexual, but who so feared the negative reactions of his world that he inhibited homosexual behavior by conscious and subconscious will, even to the degree that he erased the memories of its emergence when he failed to inhibit it. In his miraculously facile and frightened mind, he devalues homosexual behavior so completely that its reality, however powerful at the moment, becomes thoroughly buried, as if it never had happened.

The mid-range of the continuum would be populated by men who acquiesce to heterosexist ideas by marginally acknowledging some aspect of their homosexuality but still maintaining the belief that there is a moral hierarchy, a qualitative difference between what they are and what they are not, and that what they are not—heterosexual—is somehow better. Here, in order to deal with the feared loss of important heterosexual people in his life, the gay man might choose the strategy of acknowledging that his behavior is homosexual but rejecting that he is, according to Cass. In that scenario, he may continue to compartmentalize his sexuality by keeping it separate from other aspects of his life, acknowledging in private moments that he is gay and thus identifying himself as homosexual only in certain surroundings. Basically he passes for straight. The thought of the pain of inevitable losses is so intolerable that he regularly fragments his identity, following the heterosexual map all during the workday, for example, and furtively living out his homosexual needs and desires in off hours at off locations, truck stops along the interstates and railroad station lavatories, a sad creature of fear driven into shameful behavior.

In another, more flamboyantly creative, mid-range variation, he also may institutionalize the dichotomy of his life by defining himself as bisexual, and find cliques of socially avant-garde players who affirm for him that bisexuality is acceptable to them, even for those who live according to the traditional maps.

Those who manage this stage by resisting the condemnation inherent in the larger society's definition of them often find themselves in that crucible where fate and identity are forced to face each other. The first intimation of what others define as aberrant desire, whether embraced or repressed, marks the beginning of a mysteriously chronic confrontation with fate. Few who came of age in the seventies or before escape the torment of their sexual self-knowledge, and wrestling with desire may lead them to contest convention in brave and imaginative ways, because convention would deny them the logic of their existence and their existence seems to have nothing to do with rational choice. Gays thus develop a measure of respect for mystery and uncertainty, because who they are seems much further beyond their control than who is their more purely rationally heterosexual brother. It makes more sense to be heterosexual. More people are, and species perpetuation requires it. Yet I am not. Why?

It provides a constant impetus for self-examination, because it is a mystery, and mysteries do that. And since there are no real answers, the gay man experiences a sense of having fate as his companion, which is kind of a functional paradox in that it allows gays to operate fairly well with monumental uncertainty. Unlike heterosexuals, who appear to believe against all available evidence that their desires and their biological responses are universal and even right, and who therefore find no cause to examine their own sexuality, gays ultimately must be able to ponder what is, understand that it may defy their understanding, perhaps shrug, and ultimately accept and adapt.

Experiencing loss the way they do, so regularly and so profoundly, gay men become very familiar with it and its bitter aftertaste, grief. That familiarity with loss and grief also has helped gays deal with the AIDS epidemic and the mounting disappointments it so far has presented. A social and psychological upheaval is emerging from the pain and confusion and rage inspired by the epidemic—emotions already familiar to the gay boy struggling in a homophobic society.

Oppression breeds heroism, however, and resisting individually society's attempts to define with malice their sexuality obviously has led some men to engage in organized resistance as an active means for creating social change. Gay men now have provided and established many institutions to provide for those stricken with AIDS, from hotlines to hospices to educational institutions, to organizing clinical trials, procuring obscure medications, to, essentially, founding a sort of cultural revolution that makes sense of all the forces they have to deal with, surviving in a hostile world, and dealing far more bravely with the question of death.

Gay activists have propelled themselves into the vanguard of the American public health system and challenged everything about the way health care in America is organized and medical treatment delivered. Can anyone recall an incident in history wherein the mortal victims of a plague had organized and then managed to attend a mass demonstration in the nation's capital to voice their desperate opposition to the drug policies of a government that regulated the distribution of drugs they hoped might cure them? Many became members of committees and councils designing policies on how insurers, doctors, and hospitals should treat them. And at the same time, they refused to compromise the idea of their enjoying the sex of their sexuality, promoting as they did not only safer sex but safer "hot" sex.

"Despite the epidemic," say these vanguard gays, "despite the homophobia, we are not giving up who we are or how we love. We still are going to make love, and though we intend to make it safer for each other, we also intend to research and develop our lovemaking so that it is even more stimulating, more exciting, more fun and hotter than ever. We have been on the leading edge of everything else good and creative in this society. Now we are inventing new avenues for lovemaking."

Continuous fear, mourning, and even terror are part of the fabric of a gay man's life, and to become resigned to that would be to give away his life, to give away his reason for living. So organizations like Act Up and Queer Nation and all the activities of gay politics provide a concrete basis for resistance and then, presumably, hope.

Action through struggle is the essential part of every gay man's consciousness. So is questioning injustice and a familiarity with misery that leads or can lead to spirituality. Faith, for gays, is a question of operating with doubt, moving beyond doubt, and, above all, beyond self-doubt, with a much more heightened sense of fraternity and community and thus a spirituality not defined by rules, as in a religion, but by the challenges of being gay. The men who internalize society's hostility often live their lives as antisocially and despondently as the society's condemnations would reinvent them. Others rise up and accommodate and manage this stage of their development by critically examining the prejudicial definitions of themselves, reshaping those beliefs and somehow changing from negative to positive the connotation of homosexuality, allowing them to move on, despite the stated and unstated opposition, to the next stage of their growth; exploring and experimenting with living their lives under a new set of postulates and assumptions, moving toward their own eventual rebirth under an entirely new premise, with whatever combination of fear and relief they feel for having navigated the most wrenching and confusing turning points of their lives.

COMING OUT—
RITES OF
PASSAGE

Accepting homosexuality requires profound changes in the self and in social relationships. The change happens over time, through a series of successive events that help serve to deconstruct cultural ideas and lead to learning new social roles, the sum of which defines being gay.

The transition takes place in three phases.

In the first, the gay man acknowledges his feelings in private, usually to another gay man. In telling, however hesitantly, he begins the process of announcing to the world who he is, of advancing his self-definition from heterosexual to homosexual, of exploring and experimenting, while still modifying his public behavior in accordance with the responses of others.

The second phase is marked by his social debut into a small group of other gays, the beginning of his public coming out. His social identification with gay men helps to shift his self-concept

113

from *homosexual*, the dominant society's language for who he is, to *gay man*, a new defining category with its own social rules and cultural knowledge.

In the third phase, he moves from the covert world of being gay to the public world, pressing for his full right to be who he is in every circumstance, openly confronting prejudice and bigotry.

Supported by a strong sense of community, he solidifies his status as a gay man, having traveled the journey that began with feeling alienated for his different-ness and culminated in his arrival at a self-perception that made him feel proud.

Assuming a
Homosexual Identity

Exploring and Experimenting

After months of lengthy discussions with my wife, we booked a "Cruise to Nowhere" for the Memorial Day weekend. By that time my every instinct was open to self-fulfillment, my involuntary reactions as well as my conscious awareness. I was as frightened as I was eager to begin my real life but still in the process of living what rapidly was becoming my former life, writing the last chapter of it, in effect, while thinking always of the future. I loved the idea that the trip was a cruise to nowhere and billed as exactly that. It left from the West Side piers and just lolled around in the Atlantic for a couple of days.

In preparing for the trip, my wife and I went shopping for clothes and stopped specifically for me at a neighborhood men's boutique. As I entered the doorway, I locked eyes with John, the store manager. I had never seen him before. I don't recall ever having seen any man quite that way before, at least not consciously. He was lean, angular, long-limbed and lightly muscled, with a shock of thick blond hair coursing over the right side of his face. He looked at me with incredible intensity, and the magnetism between us was so palpable that, years later, my wife confessed to me that the moment she saw the two of us gaze at each other, she knew that our marriage truly was over, that it might even have ended with thundering finality at that very instant.

I bought a lot of clothes that day. John could have sold me anything and nearly did. I already was very clothes conscious, but John was particularly attentive, complimentary, even seductive, and no man was more ready than I for such a provocative sales pitch. From moment to moment in the store, I found myself reliving a version of every thunderstruck boy-meets-girl pageantry I had ever seen, read, or imagined. I watched his long fingers riffle through the racks of sport jackets like the hands of a concert pianist. If he said I might look elegant in a particular suit, I wanted immediately to try it on for him. When he measured my waist, I got chills. When he draped a jacket over my shoulders and I felt his fingertips linger and his palms smooth the jacket over my back, I closed my eyes and imagined his hands on my skin. I stared at his face when I should have been looking at the colors and fabrics he was showing me in his hand. I became woozy in the unseen smoke of his cologne. I was ossified by his attentiveness. I was from moment to moment fourteen and seventeen and nineteen years old, and something spectacularly wonderful was happening to me for the first time.

During the cruise, John monopolized my thoughts. I was completely distracted by the sensations that had been awakened within me, paramount among them the whole visceral phenomenon of love at first sight, or biochemical infatuation at first sight, whichever applied. After years of repressing my natural feelings, I was now embracing the feelings hungrily, knowing all the while that I fully intended to act consciously on the feelings rather than ignore them or wish them away, or worse, to act on them furtively, so that if I didn't repress the feelings I would repress the memories of whatever I did with them.

When my wife and I returned from the cruise, I returned to the boutique. John was there and much to my delight remembered me and everything about me, from the size of my waist to the name of the institute where I worked and precisely what I did there. He was very solicitous, and at the end of a lengthy and animated conversation we agreed to have dinner together the following Friday.

Yet another beginning.

As I began to see him more and more regularly, my absences from the apartment became increasingly meaningful to my wife. Not knowing if it would be more or less painful in the end, I chose to be completely honest with her. I told her that I was seeing John and when, that I was sharing lunches and dinners with him, talking at length with him about my life, our lives, and the direction in which I felt I was headed. I was not having a sexual relationship with him yet, and I told her that too, but it was clear to both of us, all three of us, that I wanted to explore these feelings of mine and that eventually I would have a sexual relationship with a man, and John more likely than any other. The period was very painful for my wife and more confusing to her, I'm sure, because while she was clearly in pain she also was extremely compassionate.

By late summer I had told her that I had to leave the apartment. At that point I was wildly in love with this man, or at least with my idea of him, and, although I was not consciously aware of it, I probably knew that he was my passport out of the old life and into the new one.

I moved out in July or August, to an apartment in roughly the same neighborhood. I moved from 77th Street and First Avenue to 77th and Madison, to the top floor of a brownstone, so that I would be within walking distance of my daughter.

Having deliberated and planned nearly my every move from childhood, except for a few variations that I conveniently had forgotten, I now entered a period of my life wherein I seemed to have little control at all. My conscious mind always had ruled, making certain that I followed the accepted course and stuck to the larger society's plan. Now, in allowing my true self to emerge, my unconscious was running ahead of me. For the first time in my life I honestly did not know what I was doing. Another self was going to do what it had to do to begin to catch up, make up for lost time, and I suddenly was a passenger in my own life.

The ride would prove to be exhilarating and perilous.

I began our union with an intensity equal to my prior repression. I was addicted to John, and he was a wild card. As legitimate as my life had been, his had not. I had lived between the lines; he lived on the edges. He never had held a long-term job. He had attended college and trained as a filmmaker, but he never had made a film, and he had left school a few credits shy of a degree. He had left every stage of his life a few credits shy, in fact, but he was so strikingly charming and handsome, he had managed to negotiate the days of his life without much effort. Doors opened for him.

He also was extremely mysterious and secretive, whereas I was very forthright. I suppose we were as opposite as we could be. I later recognized that he was the embodiment of freedom that I was seeking in myself. He had traveled in gay circles at every level. He knew the darkest and the brightest sides, from the piers where the cruising of modern legend went on to the inner wards of Studio 54, where the elite met, coupled, networked, and formed exotic matrices.

Gradually, and with my overenthusiastic blessing, John made his way deeper into my life. Soon he was living with me in the small but elegant new apartment.

Strangely, John held himself at arm's length from me, and —irony of ironies—he rejected me sexually more often than not. My sexual attraction for him was strong to begin with and then intensified by my barely controllable need to catch up with my own life, but my longing went largely unrequited, which more or less kept me in an ironically familiar pattern of anticipation and rejection.

I had gotten out of my marriage and seized this opportunity to live as myself. My longing for the life was intense, yet I was being rejected. Since over my lifetime I had fashioned myself into such an expert at denial, and self-denial in particular, I somehow managed to embrace a Zen-like attitude of patience, convincing myself that time and love would nurture this relationship and allow whatever was supposed to be natural to unfold in a beautiful and poetic way.

Any romantic lover who has suffered and re-examined his or her own self-degradation in "playing the fool" for love will understand what I was doing and how doomed I was. I was utterly obsessed with John, and I understood only much later that while I thought I was trying to honor myself for the first time, I was a long way from being strong and solid enough even to recognize myself. Actually, I was feeling humiliated because I still was trying to shame myself for who I was. I had ended my former life; I barely had recognized the dishonesty and the futility of it. I was a naive freshman in a new life, a plebe, an apprentice, and I had no idea of it. As far as I knew, though, I was desperately in love, passionately determined to be patient, to be stoic and to build a life with this man.

John, meanwhile, was being his best self, looking out for his best self-interests. I offered him ample opportunity. I was at the height of my career. I had begun to receive invitations to travel all over the world. John encouraged me to be more entrepreneurial about my successes. He suggested that he videotape the lectures I was giving and edit all the previously videotaped therapy sessions I had accumulated at Ackerman, and that we together form a business that would promote my work and market it separately on videotape.

I had been invited by the Catholic University and the National Institute of Mental Health to lecture and consult in Lima, Peru. It seemed natural that John would travel with me, and by winter we were off on a month-long, exotic, and highly romantic adventure. From Peru, we flew off again, this time to Mexico, then to Switzerland, then to Italy, before returning to tour the United States, John all the while making videotapes of extraordinarily poor quality because he did not know what he was doing, although I chose to ignore that completely.

John gave up all other outside work and devoted his energies to the management of my career. He booked lectures, made flight and limousine arrangements, reserved hotels, collected fees, managed bank accounts, and kept records for tax purposes.

I meanwhile worked fairly strenuously to travel and lecture, maintain my position as Director of Education at the Ackerman Institute for Family Therapy in New York, and support two households. While I was fretting and agonizing about the love of my life, I also was lecturing, administrating, seeing private patients, and visiting my daughter regularly. Because I was so obsessed with my fear of being rejected by John, I have no doubt I was being the worst father I could possibly be. With my underlying guilt, shame, and eroding self-esteem, I probably had nothing left to give her. Worse, I was hiding from her the very relationship that was robbing her of her father's attention and affection because I had not yet told her the reason I had left the marriage.

For that reason, and because I was so overwhelmed by the paradox of my wife's heroic compassion in the face of what appeared to be my self-absorption in disrupting her life, also no doubt because I felt such sub-surface shame over the underlying reason for it, I made certain not to deprive them economically. I tried to provide them with whatever I had provided for them before, while also trying to provide John with as flamboyant, elegant, and romantic a lifestyle as I could.

How frantically I built my house of cards.

In the meantime, John and I had met so many fascinating people and seen such extraordinary opportunity in Peru that we began to think seriously of moving somewhere closer to South America, perhaps Florida. While still discussing the idea, we found an absolutely amazing house for sale in Coconut Grove, a

1929 house designed and built by a famous architect, a beautiful Art Deco villa that had been renovated.

I bought it in April 1986.

There we founded the Miami Institute for Family Therapy, an international training center. I had been teaching a good deal in Miami, so I was able to develop a strong following of trainees and patients.

John moved into the house, and from April until June I remained in New York, commuting to Florida on weekends to see John and to conduct workshops. During the weeks of that spring I hustled about, taking care of the business of ending my New York practice, saying good-bye to patients, colleagues, friends and Alyssa, my daughter, and preparing to live my new and extraordinary life in Florida. On the proverbial edge.

On the night of June 24, 1986, I spoke to John on the telephone. I was flying to Florida the following day, having finished every last detail of folding up my New York life. He was on his way out to a party. We had a pleasant and lively conversation, but at the end of it he basically kissed me good-bye. I took a sort of fleeting note of it, because he never had done anything like it before.

At the airport in Florida, John was nowhere to be found. I waited a half hour before calling the house. There was no answer. With mounting anxiety I waited another half hour, then telephoned again, and, getting no answer, I took a cab to the house.

As I fumbled with the key in the lock, I could hear John's dog sniffing and barking on the other side of the door. John had adopted a mixed-breed, mostly black labrador retriever. The dog whined and shook wildly from his midsection back to his tail when I finally entered.

The house was empty.

Hollow empty.

I could see almost immediately from foyer to living room to dining room that all of John's possessions were gone, and it gradually became clear to me that most of mine were gone too. The dog had defecated in punctuation in the grand living room and in the dining room. Later, I discovered that he also had soiled a guest room too.

A house of cards and a titanic denial system have in common a tinsel strength and a longevity that is most remarkable, particularly in retrospect, but that yields totally to one great gust of the undeniable, whereupon it emulsifies in a microsecond.

I collapsed.

I knew in a storm of sudden mental outtakes that he was gone and that my new world and my new life and my old life too were gone, and that the plantation in my mind had burned to the ground, and that I was a fool, a colossal fool, and that I had lost all power and ability to judge or decide or move forward or backward.

As I wandered from that day into the next and the next, I learned among other appropriately painful lessons about John, to whom I had turned over all of the details of my life, that he had not paid the bills, that he had not been paying the bills, either in New York or Florida.

Then, as anyone else might already have suspected, I learned that John had been using my credit cards; then that he had been using them liberally; then that he was continuing to use my credit cards, as bill after bill fell day after day onto the floor of the foyer from the mail slot, including one for hundreds of dollars worth of shoes purchased at Saks in New York on June 27, three days after he had left.

I teetered on the brink of despondency. I had lost the person I believed I loved in an epic way. My possessions were gone. Such fortune as I had was gone. My heart was gone. I had left behind my family, my practice, my past, my reputation, and all that was familiar to me. I was alone in a grand, unfamiliar and cavernously empty house. I felt shame and humiliation like I had never before imagined, let alone experienced. I had no confidence whatsoever in my judgment. I questioned my decisions to open the mail, to answer the telephone, to call a friend or an acquaintance, or to postpone the call. From moment to moment

I tortured myself with the vivid memories of hundreds of moments and details that I had noticed and not taken note of, heard and not heeded, sensed and not responded to: hasty gestures, evasive answers, empty suggestions, excuses, explanations, rationalizations, patronizing flattery and lies and lies and lies; subtle, boldfaced, clever, brazen, plain, elaborate, cruel, cute, novel, repetitive, artistic, and mundane.

Of course the signs were there; signs were strewn everywhere. Billboards. I was just stupid. I had no eyes for signs. I had no judgment. I could not trust myself to tell a cop from a mugger, a boat from a building. Here I was, great, renowned expert in human behavior and mental illness, and not only was I an emotional pile of ruins, I could not trust my own judgment.

Maybe a week into this mock epic self-condemnation, I received a call from a friend whom John and I had met in Italy and to whom I regurgitated the entire sordid story. He hesitated for a somber moment and then told me that he knew of at least two other instances in which John had behaved similarly, in different parts of the country, of course. I could not even decide if I should take comfort in the new knowledge or feel more deeply insulted.

Another week or two droned by, and a young man knocked at my door and asked if I would be willing to allow him to use the house as a location for an episode of the television series *Miami Vice*. They would pay $1,500 a day. I wept with relief after he left. I had no money, and I could not work, since my skills all were wrapped up in my judgment, and I had proven that I had no judgment.

I invited my daughter to come down for the *Miami Vice* shooting. I thought she would appreciate the glamour and the excitement. My wife followed shortly thereafter, having either detected my emotional distress over the telephone or heard convincing word of it from Alyssa. My wife had decided to move away from New York too. They were going to California. When she arrived in Florida, she saw that I was a mess. She was very sympathetic. It was very comforting. It felt as if they were my only connection to a stable and familiar world.

After they left, I tried to put my life back together and soon realized that I could not. I simply could not. I was torn from all my anchors. I trusted nothing. I had to reconcile myself with two betrayals: first, in living a lie for so long, then, the betrayal into which I had so willingly waltzed.

Within a few months the bank foreclosed on the house and whatever dreams I had invested in it. My wife and Alyssa moved to Mill Valley, California, near San Francisco. I followed, settling in the city itself, where I began a long period of retreat and recovery. I also began, in earnest, a process of becoming who I was supposed to become, alternately on three fronts: becoming gay, becoming a man, and becoming a gay man.

If John had been my passport and, I guess, my shield from too harsh a transition into gay culture and the gay community, I now had to negotiate all of that for myself without any protection, which is one way I had used him while he was using me. I had to learn a new language and set of rules for a culture and community outside the obvious rules.

I was fortunate to be invited to teach at the University of California at Berkeley. I had sent my résumé around and gotten a call out of the blue one day that they needed a teacher in family therapy. They knew my work and asked me if I was available, and of course I was. In fact, the position offered a perfect solution to my professional inertia and self-doubt. I could now lean on my experience and knowledge without fear. I could teach family therapy without having to risk failure at practicing it. I would be tapping my memory and passion for sharing what I had learned. I would not be straining to resurrect my fallen self-confidence, would not be calling upon my talent, my instincts, my imagination, or my tarnished judgment.

As part of my willingness to dive into the depths of my grief from the deconstruction of my heterosexual life and from the betrayal, I found myself working on an AIDS unit as the bereavement therapist. I don't think my motivation was entirely self-flagellating, but I suspect that an element of penance was present. I like to think that a more profound curiosity was motivating me, that my inspiration was more an attempt to understand the true meaning of grief and to engage in a process with the grieving, partly because I believed I could help, given my vast clinical background, and because I believed I could learn from the stricken, certainly to put my own sadness and fear in perspective, which proved to be true.

I thereby bypassed once again the issue of trusting my judgment. I was becoming an expert in grieving, not in dealing with how to make a relationship successful. It was a natural bridge. I was in the throes of grief and could empathize. I certainly was not in the throes of any successful relationship. I had barely survived my first homosexual relationship and in retrospect, I understand that it served to dismantle my former self more than to provide a foundation for my emerging, authentic self.

But first relationships frequently serve precisely that purpose. Many gay men who have led heterosexual lives have constructed elaborate strategies to support their own self-denial and to deceive their community as well. Often their first homosexual relationships provide the dramatic opportunity to dismantle those structures—in extreme cases, like mine, to demolish them—and start anew.

Coming out at this stage requires the unlearning and the deconstruction of irrelevant cultural ideas as much as the learning of new rules and roles. Such transformations involve the body, mind, and soul, a restructuring of personhood and a new view of his social surroundings, going beyond the previous stage, *self-identification*, in which primarily a cognitive change takes place. As a gay man goes through the process of unlearning heterosexist rules and becoming socialized into a self-affirming gay cultural system with new and open relationships, each successive relationship and social experience sums up and confirms his increasingly positive gay identity, usually in confrontation with stigma and discrimination.

Despite such creativity as they demonstrate and adaptive strategies they invent, gay men enter the stage of identity assumption and presentation dreadfully pained and awkward. Much more so than their heterosexual counterparts, they are unsure of nearly every encounter, except for the certainty of some degree of rejection. Those who postpone their acknowledgment and who delay presenting their gay selves to the world later proceed with an agony and insecurity that only increases as they procrastinate making the passage.

Recognizing or merely feeling the need for external affirmation, writes Eli Coleman, the gay man eventually takes a chance and risks revealing himself, hoping against all he so far has learned that his confidant will not reject or condemn him. To boost the odds in his favor, he begins the process by selecting another gay man or gay men as his audience.

Naturally, the first person in whom he confides wields over him the threatening power of betrayal and thus can have a colossal impact on whatever he might think, feel, or do next, and maybe for the rest of his life. If the person responds negatively, he or she may confirm all the negative impressions and reinforce all the low self-concepts the developing gay man already has nurtured, and thereby hinder or halt the development of a positive self. If the reaction is positive, which is likelier these days than it was even a decade ago, the developing gay man will begin gradually to become more comfortable with his same-sex feelings and their social and emotional implications.

Does it seem exaggerated to suggest that a single encounter, a solitary wager of trust or ego might so profoundly affect an entire life? Self-images that have run so many gauntlets and skirted so many perils are fabulously fragile.

The possibilities for relative success or failure in the presentation of the gay self compose a limitless spectrum of scenarios of pain and loss on the one end, and triumph and relief on the other. How many terrified gay souls have crawled back into psychic hiding or suffered painful developmental setbacks because of the mocking reactions of homophobic men and women—whichever their sexuality—in whom they confided? Or, how many gay men teetering on the brink of permanent self-condemnation were rescued by the gracious sensitivity of a non-judgmental friend, acquaintance or family member, homosexual or otherwise?

The connection to a gay context usually results in increased self-esteem. That in turn leads to really accepting a homosexual identity, which will be the next stage.

Emotional and sexual experimentation marks this connection and therefore this period, according to Coleman. The gay man who passes through this stage successfully begins to heal his wounds and allow himself to indulge an increasing sense of "normalcy" about his homosexuality. *Normal* combined with *homosexual* at first may sound like an oxymoron to him, but inasmuch as he accepts and experiences evidence that he is a part of a demographic reality in every generation of human beings, in every corner of the globe, the developing gay man will begin to realize that he is representative of a consistent statistical constituency, and that he therefore is quite normal. Being different immediately becomes less weird and terrifying upon the discovery of a whole world of people who share the same difference.

Once he assumes membership in this unfamiliar world, the emerging gay man is bound by all his natural curiosity and longing to explore it socially, emotionally, and sexually.

Adaptive Strategies

The bridge between identifying himself as gay and presenting himself as gay represents a crucial rite of passage for the developing gay man, especially since so few meaningful rites exist in his life.

Individuals in this stage of development face the task of telling other people who they are and then awaiting the consequences, which they justifiably expect to be dire. In order even to approach this stage, explains Vivienne Cass, the gay man has to recognize the sexual, social, and emotional needs that go with being homosexual. He needs contact and community in a world that condemns both, as far as he knows. He is practically blind to the possibility that the whole coming-out process actually can serve to heal the injuries of societal prejudice and his internalization of those prejudices, and that it may begin to restore a sense of integrity and well-being for his damaged self.

Homosexual sexual exploration is in itself an adaptive strategy toward this end. With it the individual leads himself into the formation of his first gay relationships, which are as important to his maturation as the straight young man's first heterosexual relationships.

His homosexual development will take him where sex will not appear to have been designed to go. In earlier stages he became involved first with sex play, which was innocent. Then, when recognizing that for him sex with a man had an emotional component that distinguished him from his heterosexual buddies, it was a little more complex than innocent. Now, in this stage, he will learn to make a unique intellectual shift or adjustment regarding the connection between sex and emotion, because assuming a gay identity requires tremendous flexibility regarding sex and emotion. The sexually participating gay must be able to maintain the sexual-emotional connection when sex serves a communicative purpose, and also be able to suspend the relationship between sex and emotion for the unfamiliar new occasions when sex either serves a self-identifying purpose or serves no familiar purpose whatsoever, except the pure enjoyment of itself.

Sexual experimentation for a developing gay man requires that he view sex from an entirely different philosophical perspective than his background has allowed him. A fundamentally intellectual readjustment, it is fraught with varying layers of emotional fear, hesitation, guilt, and regret. But it makes sense.

And, by the way, no heterosexual in this society can expect to shed his prejudices against gays unless he or she first understands the logic of sexuality from the gay premise.

All the theorems and postulates the emerging gay man—

and everyone else as well—has learned and accepted about sex are rooted in the heterosexist notion that heterosexuality is the only form of sexual practice that makes any sense: the human male is constructed sexually to enter a woman and deposit the seeds that fertilize the makings of the next generation; the female is constructed along a plan that permits such entry by the male and offers for such fertilization an ovum eager to be fertilized and join the next generation of humans.

Therefore, the logical argument proceeds, opposite-gender sexuality is normal and good most of the time, and any other kind of sexuality is abnormal all of the time.

To that admittedly simplified secular equation, religions have added or subtracted varying degrees of relativity regarding normalcy, acceptability, responsibility, spirituality and even the extent to which indulgence in procreative activity should be enjoyable or, for that matter, enjoyed.

More often than not, religions have valued sex primarily for its procreative results, secondarily for its communicative value, and, in the main, not at all for such pleasures as it affords the participants. Orthodoxies of varying stripes have attempted to convince or coerce their congregants to hide, erase, disguise, or eliminate the pleasure inherent in sexual activity, and at the very least to keep to themselves about it. Depending on the religion, clerics have ascribed wide-ranging moral values to the heights and depths of sexual achievement, a precious few religions actually extolling the attainment of such ecstasy as true ardor mixed with caring effort might produce—most, however, condemning it. In fact, many religions strongly suggest a divine equation linking spiritual purity with sexual deprivation and spiritual depravity with sexual indulgence, not to mention enjoyment.

Hence, a plethora of slogans, aphorisms, credos and admonitions that continually contradict one another on human nature, whichever comes first: Go thou and multiply. Virginity equals purity. Reading *Playboy* can be an "occasion of sin." The sole purpose of sex is to have children. "Knowledge," or experience, equals promiscuity, equals perversion, equals evil. Women should wear veils to hide their allure. Women should wear hats in church. The president lusted in his heart. Polygamy is wrong except for certain males and some deliciously mythical Amazons. Prostitution, found wherever there is ambient air, is morally wrong. The Blessed Mother Mary was a virgin when she delivered Jesus and either remained a virgin or is no longer a proper subject of discussion, though the purpose of marriage is children and their denial is grounds for annulment. Mary Magdalene was a lowly sinner, Diana and Venus, goddesses. Onan wasted his seed, though probably not the first time, when he likely lost it nocturnally, without meaning to, and the rhythm method is an acceptable method of birth control.

Nearly all religions uniformly condemn sexuality that does not conform to the apparent logic their founders and apologists observed and interpreted in the polarity designed into the two sexes. Nearly all leave out the possibility and in fact ignore the overwhelming evidence that in a global percentage of their population, the chemical-emotional magnetism simply is reversed: positive can be and in fact is attracted to positive and negative to negative, in spite of the equipment design, in spite of the engineering plan, and against the logic that proceeds so flawlessly from the heterosexist premise until it arrives at the conclusion that all people will feel, sexually, the way they appear to have been constructed to feel.

Simply put, not all people feel that way. Not all biochemical-emotional systems work precisely in conjunction with the visible procreative design. Some people's feelings—in fact, those of a consistently repeating percentage—are diametrically opposite their design specifications, making the fundamental procreative premise irrelevant to them and thus requiring them to think—and live—according to a psychosexual system that proceeds from a different premise, one emotionally unfamiliar to heterosexuals: that sex does not necessarily have a primarily procreative purpose, that for people whose biochemical urges do not conform to their procreative design, sex is more a language or even a recreation than it is a means to a species-perpetuating end; that as a form of expression or recreation, sex therefore can be as profound as a passionate proclamation of loyalty, devotion, and love when the participants so determine, or as meaningless and playful as a polite salutation. It can be a powerful expression of ardor—or a way to kill an hour while waiting for the cable television repair crew. Viewed from a premise that by biological necessity devalues procreation and instead values expression and play, sex does not have to be an important part of the relationship or an important part of the morning. It does not have to be important at all. It does not have to be fraught with meaning, though it certainly can be. It does not require emotional maturity nor even an emotional connection, and certainly not a commitment—though, if the participants agree, it certainly can do that too. It does not necessarily require privacy, then, though it can; nor a numerical limitation on the participants, though it can; or any limitations whatsoever on the details or frequency of its indulgence; or any prior introductions, or a cigarette afterward. Homosexual sex does not require rules, nor are the heterosexual rules relevant to it in any remote way. Homosexual sex requires only the abandonment of irrelevant restrictions, assumptions, suppositions, fears, and judgments.

Heterosexual moral judgments about sexual behavior do not apply to homosexual sexuality, nor does the attendant highly charged immoral definition of promiscuity, which also is tied to the sociopolitical structure of a publicly monogamous relationship, marriage, which our society denies gays anyway.

In order to survive, the emerging gay man has to jettison all these irrelevant religious, moral, and ethical constructs and invent or embrace a new view of sexuality, perhaps as an element in a process of self-discovery and affirmation wherein he permits himself to claim another piece of his own identity through each sexual or even asexual encounter. For his survival and development, and while heterosexuals paradoxically are condemning him for what they view as his obsession with sex, the emerging homosexual must see sex as an ingredient and an instrument in his development and not as its definition.

So, with a gradually solidifying commitment to a homosexual identity, the developing gay man now seeks out other gay people and a gay culture, namely, the people in the gay subculture. His growing involvement with the gay community offers him the opportunity for support among others who understand and share his same concerns. He encounters new opportunities to meet partners. He has access to positive role models and more and more opportunities to get comfortable in a gay environment. He learns, consciously or subconsciously, that nobody can heal a damaged self-concept alone, and as he encounters others of his kind, he takes more risks.

During this period of exploration, explains Eli Coleman, the developing gay individual faces several rudimentary developmental tasks, the first of which is to learn the interpersonal skills required to meet and socialize with others of his sexual inclination. Having been socialized as heterosexual from earliest childhood, he lacks the skills to develop a same-sex relationship that includes sex as a means of communication or even as a leisure activity. As part of those skills, he will have to learn as well to develop a sense of personal attractiveness and sexual competence at a level and an intensity that might never have occurred to him before. The sexuality with which he already was familiar included certain accepted areas and levels of competition for the attentions of the potential participants; this new sexuality, which admits to its playfulness and embraces its recreational value, can be fiercely competitive and therefore quite painfully rude to its apprentices. And third, like any person in the adolescent stage of growth, the individual must learn, and most learn the hard way, that his self-esteem is not going to be dependent or even remotely related to the number of his sexual triumphs or, should he choose to view it thus, his sexual conquests.

Like the prototypical randy adolescent, the gay man at this stage is ready to have sex with a variety of partners, and he is eager. The way has been cleared for him to so indulge too, inasmuch as potential partners abound who are either in or entering the same stage of gay development with an eagerness borne of the same history of sexual repression.

Biological traditions like high sex drives, easily triggered responsiveness, and the species history of the sexual chase seem to exist in exaggerated form in men. Women do not seem so driven and usually require psychological preparation. Whereas it might be considered unusual behavior for a woman, it is not at all unusual that gay men make sex partner choices with seemingly little discrimination and often for purely sexual reasons. "Not denying a biological substrata, males are taught to see sex in active, genital-focused and goal-oriented terms," according to J. L. Laws and P. Schwartz, writing in *Sexual Scripts: The Social Construction of Female Sexuality.* "Females are encouraged to view sexuality in interactive, emotionally focused, and process-oriented ways."

Still, even the process of cruising, or selecting a sexual partner, is deeper and more complex than it appears. It usually involves not only checking out the sexual readiness of total strangers but screening them carefully—if subconsciously—for particular aspects that might satisfy the cruiser's fantasy while actually blocking out distracting details of who or what the person actually is. The process of claiming your forbidden homosexual identity involves getting to know many hidden parts of your undiscovered self through these initial, temporary attractions to strangers. A prospective partner momentarily alluring for his especially masculine demeanor may be caressing the nerve endings of that part of the homosexual self that wishes to test its most feminine attributes. At another time a more feminine man may stir exactly the opposite instincts and urging within the same self. Acquiescing to the attraction (a more judgmental and therefore negatively charged phrase might suggest "yielding to the temptation") allows the untried, unexplored traits to awaken, stretch, examine, and explore their own existence.

By the time he emerges from this exploratory experimental

period, a gay man may have probed every possible variation of himself, using his sexuality as, forgive the expression, a divining rod. A gay man who spends any time reflecting on his history of cruising always will recall some quality about one or another of his sexual partners that allowed him to get in touch with some hidden or underdeveloped part of himself. The sexual partner's real identity in most of these liaisons almost always is irrelevant in the face of the comparatively towering significance of the identity he allows the gay explorer to discover within himself.

Paco, a twenty-eight-year-old raised in Ecuador by his American-born mother and his Ecuadoran father, an oral surgeon, was himself educated in the United States and dropped out of medical school to become an artist, photographer, and filmmaker. Simultaneously he was acknowledging and exploring his homosexuality, and through a variety of important sexual relationships he progressively learned about who he was. "Louie was the person with whom my body freed itself," he said. "Until then I didn't know the erogenous points in my body. Louie understood every one. The experiences I had with men up to then were all genital-centered. Louie awakened me, my chest, my legs, my skin. For the first time I made love. There were times in the past when the physical and emotional came together, but with him it felt complete, the union between emotional and physical. He was able to help me get through all the physical barriers, all the shields I had constructed. Despite my shyness, despite my fears, I succeeded in falling into a space with Louie that was completely comfortable. Sexuality became a private refuge.

"After Louie, I had an affair with a priest. The fantasy I explored with him was about possession. I see myself as a giving person. I did throughout my childhood and throughout this affair. This priest totally desired me. And through his desire I allowed him to possess me. There was enormous power in my surrendering, but not in the conventional sense of power. I didn't have it; I gave it up, but in giving it up, I became powerful. It was about total giving, in the extreme. It offered me complete freedom, as I had nothing left to lose. I suddenly felt able to go anywhere mentally. I could get away from all rationalization, from all the restrictions of reason.

"Later, I met a painter, Juan, who admired my being. With Juan the freedom was in knowing how completely he wanted me. It was not necessarily physical. It seemed more about symbols, about learning to be an object. We would be in an apartment surrounded by paintings, and everything would become extremely intense. Everything would lose its name—book, painting, Paco—we were all objects of his desire.

"With Lee all of the elements have been brought together. I trust him. He is from a family of intellectuals. Though our politics are different, we complement each other. He completes me. We have the same experience, even the same body shape. We're both uncircumcised. When I see him, and when I make love to him, it's like I'm loving myself."

Over time, and after numerous sexual exchanges, the gay man evolves sexually and realizes more clearly who he is sexually. That helps him re-create himself socially, then ethically, and ultimately as a fully integrated, psychologically maturing gay man, all of which makes this exploration stage largely a transitional one in which men are more or less searching for themselves as well as for a partner with whom they might strike up a more lasting kind of relationship. The association with other gays humanizes and universalizes the developing gay man's sexuality. For the first time he is among others who are essentially just like him, and the affiliation gradually results in a developmental reparation of his social skills, talents, and all that was lost during his very conflicted and dangerous adolescence. Of course, it is unavoidable that from time to time during such transitional stages, he will encounter the opposite of the support he so eagerly craves and desperately needs to effect these reparations, and as he confronts the negative influences, he is likely to backslide, to devalue the subculture that can best rescue him.

Perils abound, always.

More commonly, though, he internalizes the encouragement and the approval offered in social and sexual exploration until in time it becomes self-esteem, assertiveness, and eventually self-acceptance. Similarly, he refashions the grandiosity and exhibitionism associated with his adolescent-like behavior into feelings of vitality and vibrancy. And in identifying with the larger homosexual community, he derives feelings of empowerment, replacing the fears, feelings of loss, and powerlessness that so overwhelmed him earlier. He also receives guidance and comfort, throughout his exploration. He gradually incorporates the values and the ideals of the larger community, particularly self-determination, into his personality structure, which is ever maturing and self-healing. For those who deal well with the exploration strategies, an important shift will occur in this stage: his "significant others" are now becoming homosexuals rather than heterosexuals, and the commitment to a gay identity is now strong enough for the person to be thinking of himself as a homosexual.

Early Relationships

Generally, men at this stage are attracted to a particular set of physical and psychological traits. If a man manages to find the sought-after traits in a partner who returns his affections, he may find himself feeling irretrievably bound to that partner, almost regardless of how unbalanced the relationship may later become. I think this is probably distinct to gay relationships. It is as if the power of the original meshing forms a nearly indestructible attachment that continues to sustain the relationship despite later disappointments and conflicts. I suspect that with gays more than heterosexuals, the first leap is the greatest leap. It certainly was in my case.

A person can be enthralled by a consort who hardly has more in his favor than that he is the first sexual partner, particularly if he makes his grand, romantic entry into the individual's life after the individual has survived a long, protracted struggle with self-denial and all its attendant fears. Frequently, if not always, a gay man's first real attachment is naive and uninhibited, an all-out commitment that he likely never will match again for its intensity, bravery, and carelessness—or its disappointment, melodrama, and tragedy. First relationships are characterized by intensity, possessiveness, blind trust, and the yearning for intimacy so long denied that the resultant obsession could easily create a kind of desperation, writes Coleman—"I don't care what it takes, I'm going to make this work"—wherein the individual is passionately determined to realize an emotional Xanadu beyond what anyone could provide. It rarely settles into a realistic relationship.

Later relationships develop differently, more carefully, perhaps more sanely and less dramatically and over more time, as the experiences of love affairs bring greater self-regard.

Homosexual relationships, those deeper than the first anyway, tend to be marked by a high degree of rapport, essentially because the participants are so remarkably similar, far more similar, obviously, than participants of opposite sexes. It ought to go without saying that lovers of the same gender will have much more in common than heterosexual lovers—in attitude, in remembered experiences, in response to all varieties of stimuli.

During the experience of first relationships, however, it is the traditional heterosexist social mores—not yet the gay man's own singular creativity—that guides a gay man and shapes his expectations both of himself and his relationship, in terms of categorical issues like leadership and financial responsibility, as well as specific details like division of labor and sexual roles. Because of the natural and conditioned similarities between the two parties, the old rules, designed in however sexist a fashion to create compatibility between members of opposite genders, soon present more opportunities for competition and conflict than they do for compromise and cooperation. This conflict and competition forces the gay partners to rewrite the bylaws about leadership and to creatively reinvent the whole design of a relationship.

Invariably, as the parties struggle to negotiate nearly every event and experience, the effort becomes a continuous source of encouragement for creativity in the ever changing life. Here, at first, naïve gay men share conventional logic and even may judge themselves through conventional eyes, as they find themselves shaken daily by their own inclinations to act like conventional members of opposite genders, either by doing the laundry or being on the bottom, whichever feels most natural at the moment. As the relationship develops, so will they, until they have so rewritten the old map, they will have invented a structure for a relationship tailored very specifically to who they are and how they relate personally to each other.

Nothing is sacred in this reinvention. Depending on the individuals involved, every tradition is likely to appear for review before the board members of the relationship (whether, by the way, the members are a couple, or more than two participants, or more than three). Every time-honored characteristic of, say, a traditional marriage is subject to alteration, including, for example, the expectation for monogamy.

If a gay relationship is to last past the original fascination, it has to be flexible enough to face conflicts with the kind of honesty, openness, respect, and strength that would allow for reexaminations of issues even as sacrosanct as that of fidelity within a relationship.

Since gays include sexuality in their lives under an entirely different philosophical premise, i.e., not primarily procreative, or conforming (or allowed to conform) to an accepted religious orthodoxy, they invariably wind up proceeding very differently with the issues of sexual exclusivity and fidelity. They already have accepted that for nearly all members of their newfound gay community, sex is not significant in the same way as it is to heterosexuals. If gays amend their philosophical approach to sex so they can separate it at will from emotional attachment, then sex outside the relationship can be as benign as racquetball outside the relationship. Sexual fidelity can be unimportant, while emotional fidelity remains important. Trust remains important, open communication and honesty, not necessarily sexual fidelity.

For many people who feel a lingering loyalty to the powerful pull of the old standards, that concept requires carefully side-stepping any vow of sexual fidelity as part of the contract with each other, even if it means retooling expectations to create an imaginative psychic compromise, like including outside sexual contact in the relationship but excluding outside emotional attachment; or, more imaginatively, engaging together in non-emotional outside sexual contact, involving other more exotic arrangements—threesomes, foursomes, or orgy dates. Such experience requires tremendous personal security and trust in a relationship, which gay men achieve as they develop through the life cycle.

Because first relationships often begin before an individual's passage through a developmental stage like exploration actually is completed, the relationship may put pressure on the person to move faster ahead in his development than he actually is able, demanding commitment to a relationship before a gay man actually has committed to himself and accepted himself. That becomes a recipe for trouble, says Coleman, and some people end relationships just to relieve that pressure and to slow down the process. As unnecessarily heartbreaking as inaugurating and dissolving high-risk emotional relationships may appear, a gay man must remember that at this stage, these first relationships are part of a process. They tend to be transitional and therefore are incubators of great learning. Their rewards and tithes include great extremes of feeling, leading to greater depth and breadth of growth and understanding.

In a casual conversation Josh, an ostensibly serious and studious man in his late twenties, describes a classic first gay relationship. "It started off whirlwind with Robert," he said breathlessly. "I would see him every night, right from the beginning. It was overwhelming. He was older and he had some money, so we were able to do some extravagant things, going out to dinner at nice places all the time. He had his own apartment. I had a roommate. He was an adult, by my lights, and he was a role model for me as well as a lover. We were together for two months when I had to go away for a summer job. Until then we were together every night, and every night was incredibly intense. He came to visit me several times that summer at my job. We would have these wonderful, romantic times. It was like the fantasy of what a first love would be like, in any book, in any story in any milieu. He wrote me wonderful love letters every day. At the end of the summer, I went back, and we started seeing each other again all the time.

"Because this was my first experience, I was putting everything into it. I became very demanding. Nothing was enough for me. I wanted all of him all of the time. This was exactly what I wanted. So I felt I had to get it all. I got very angry at him because he wasn't always satisfying me in every way. I wanted him to read my mind, anticipate my needs or my emotions rather than my having to say where my head was or what I wanted. I would get ridiculously angry. An event happened some months later. I honestly don't remember now what the details were, but I just exploded, and I rejected him. I walked out. I dated on and off a little bit, but then he called me, and I thought the call was just the spark I needed. We went out again. But it only lasted about a weekend. The same pattern started over again. And we got into a fight, and it finally ended.

"I went out a lot that summer, having flings, one-night stands, for weeks too. Some months passed, and I met the second guy and I became involved with him for a longer period of time, for about a year. Joe was his name. It was a more realistic experience. It wasn't this overwhelmed, uncomfortable kind of love. I had learned through Robert that gay men can do this, that gay men can really love each other. More than anything else, I learned that it can be painful, bad even, but real.

"One of the things that had attracted me to Robert was that he was such a man. For me that still meant normal. He was the opposite of the gay stereotype. My next relationship, Joe, was with someone who was masculine and feminine. He was comfortable with both. As I became more comfortable with myself, that was less important to me, which side of himself a man preferred. In my best relationships I like the characteristics from both sides."

After John's departure I remained alone in Miami for a short while, keeping some contact with friends but feeling too confused and despondent to imagine making a home for myself there as a single gay man.

I had vaulted into a committed gay relationship before I even understood who I was, before I'd had any experience at being a gay man. The relationship with John merely substituted for the kind of marriage I was familiar with, because that was my only reference. For me, being gay still was the same as being straight, except for the gender of my sexual partner, a common and wrong-headed concept that leaves out an entire cultural, biological, psychological panorama.

I was only beginning to learn all this, and the proverbial hard way.

Too frightened to return to New York—partly because I was afraid that John would be there in body, spirit, or both, and even imagining that he sort of owned the place—I thought I would head for San Francisco, where I could be near my daughter and my ex-wife. My family.

Before making the final decision to move there, I flew out to look for a job. Thus, in the spring of 1987, I was in San Francisco, fumbling my way through this vaguely young-adult-like period of life as a man nearing forty. When I arrived for my visit, hordes of handsome gay men literally lined the streets of the predominantly gay Castro district and were visible in great numbers all during the three or four days I remained there. Handsome, athletic gay men and lesbians seemed to be everywhere, many of the men, especially, extraordinarily attractive. A city populated by brigades of gay men seemed too good to be true, and I did not know what to make of it, having not yet summoned the imagination to conjure a fantasy so unrealistic and charming. I did not know either that San Francisco was playing host that weekend to the first Gay Olympics ever, now called the Gay Games, and I was dismayed and puzzled upon my return weeks later to find the streets of San Francisco lined only with the sidewalks of San Francisco, plus a few stray residents strolling about as if for effect.

The streets were especially empty that year, in fact, because of the massive and mounting death toll due to the AIDS plague, about which I soon would be learning plenty.

Mitigating my disappointment was the success I'd had in finding a charming Victorian house to rent and a job teaching family therapy at Berkeley. Adding to it, on the other hand, in a profound and less self-absorbed way, was the communal sadness of a city grieving for its virus-besieged citizens, the dead and the dying.

Without much that was familiar to me, and still grieving deeply for the loss of John, which in turn had restimulated a wealth of regret and loss over the ending of the marriage, I now settled into a new city, a gay mecca, alone and without a passport or a guide.

It seemed appropriate for me to set about exploring and experimenting, and I did, unfortunately applying many of the heterosexual rules I knew, which were the only ones I knew.

Not knowing how to cruise, or even what cruising was precisely, I would meet a man in a bar and nearly stammer for the insecurity I felt. I did not know how long to hold a gaze or how to interpret one returned. I did not know if I was to approach someone who seemed to be gazing at me or wait until he approached me. I felt tremendously insecure and fragile, as if I were clad in a cumbersome, masculine code that was both out of style and out of season. At times I wanted simply to ask a total stranger outright, "Who makes the first move?" but I did not know how to clarify the question.

"I mean, the man or the man?"

I made the first move quite a few times and was rejected about as many times as not, but I found myself struggling even more desperately with how bad I felt when somebody else made the first move and I was not attracted to him. It was a new perspective. I did not feel compelled to respond, but I did feel obligated to communicate my disinterest so that the other man would no longer be wasting his time or feel that much more disappointed when I finally did communicate my disinterest. I knew about being rejected, as a suitor or a pursuer, and I was willing to play the percentages as I had as a young man in the dutiful pursuit of women. But I had no references in my background for the art of rejecting a suitor or the protocol for discouraging one. Also, I never before had felt the very different heat of being pursued, which gave me a whole new perspective on women in the so-called singles scene, clinging to the herd like fawns while the predators circled.

I did not know how to ask a man out on a date, nor did I know that no traditional formal structure existed anyway for asking someone out on a date. There were no actual dates, I eventually learned, and there wasn't much in the way of formal asking either.

The way of that world was much more casual than any world with which I was familiar, and I often reflect on how naïve and even odd I must have appeared to the cognoscenti, not going home at the end of an evening with someone to whom I had been talking and paying exclusive attention, but instead asking him for a date on a future evening, as if a rule existed against going home now, tonight, this minute. Those were not the rules anymore.

Very uncomfortable, unfamiliar, and awkward, I still was operating with the rules for heterosexual behavior and thinking of sexual liaisons from a heterosexual premise, assuming, for example, that sex and emotion were inextricably linked and that I would have to know something about and even like a sexual partner before I would take my clothes off in front of him; and that to indulge in any sexual activity without some kind of emotional connection was somehow morally wrong. Any number of people and institutions had taught me so, and I had learned my lessons well.

It's just that they no longer applied. This was not a society predicated on the same teachings; it acknowledged that mandating an emotional connection as a prerequisite for a serendipitous, purely physical liaison was superfluous and inhibiting, useless and even reactionary. It was more self-denial for its own sake than a self-disciplinary instrument for growth. I had to accept that experimentation more likely would lead to growth, not denial, hesitation, or superficial protocol. Risk in the face of uncertainty had a better chance of leading to some growth.

I began to attend meetings of various organizations. I joined a gay fathers' support group. I even attended services at a gay synagogue. I felt no real identification as a congregant or a member, but I was comforted by yet another meeting place and the scheduled regularity of going there and finding people. A friend of mine in New York gave me names and telephone numbers of men she knew in San Francisco, and as a result of contacting them, I was invited to a few parties, which helped, day by day. I met gay men from all different backgrounds, classes, educations and occupations, which I later learned is a refreshing characteristic of how the gay community mixes. I was generally well received at the parties, and I appreciated that, but it also was clear to me that I knew precious little about the gay culture or its language. I did not have a subtext at my disposal for references about such matter-of-factly accepted metaphors as those involving, for instance, Judy Garland or Bette Midler. Camp references passed over my ignorant head so often that I began to feel like an alien.

Having grown up in a heterosexual environment, where friends came second to family in trust and dependency relationships, I also felt my underpinnings jarred by the realization that these were people who had formed concentric circles of friends who related in a more familial way than did their blood relatives, an intimate and seemingly lifelong way, as if the members could commit no atrocity that would disenfranchise them from one another. I had not ever depended on friends to any great extent, not even in a male-bonding, softball team, lunch-box, corner-saloon way. For all those exchanges of strength and trust I depended on my wife and my extended family. These gay people depended very much on each other, and in their dependency I detected a different kind of generosity than what they offered the rest of the world and a different set of expectations, which I found confusing when its benefits came my way.

About my third month living there, when I already had been teaching and working in an AIDS unit as the bereavement therapist, I attended a gay fathers' meeting, where I met a man whom I grew to consider my coming-out buddy. Louis had been in a similar family situation, married for longer than I, and with a daughter, and he felt at least as awkward and inexperienced as I did. With each other's support, we began to experiment with what this gay life was all about. We went to bars together. We gave each other comfort and encouragement. We talked about what the rules were and what we ought to and ought not to do. We became like war buddies. We sojourned to Los Angeles and in the course of a two-day visit stayed up all night going from bar to bar until we found one of the last bathhouses open, a place where men easily had casual sexual encounters with multiple partners. The experience was simultaneously shocking and fascinating, where real animal rules seemed to apply, where the adage that if it feels good, you do it actually prevailed. Louis and I would do these things and thereafter be astonished that we had and talk about the experience for hours.

Eventually, both of us did meet men whom we dated in the more traditional way. Both of us began to separate sex from emotional attachment, generally speaking, and then separate them specifically, enjoying sex both as a recreation that was part of our lives and as a means of expressing affection and attachment when we wanted it to. I had begun first to indulge in gay sexual fantasies in my imagination and then to indulge them in my life, a conversion I never had thought possible and suddenly wondered why not. What could be more attainable, after all, than the realization of a tender fantasy about making love with a similarly inclined romantic partner?

Time and personal development plodded on, and because

I was beginning to feel not so alone in the gay world and to play out some of my fantasies, I found myself freed from the desperation and urgency of loneliness. After some time I met a considerably younger man with whom I had a three-month affair, which, unlike my relationship with John, included a certain degree of reason and realism to it. I knew it was not going to be a permanent relationship, or even terribly long-lasting, but I knew I was going to learn a great deal from it, including new lessons about enduring the dissolution of a romantic relationship without dissolving myself. I think my towering achievement during this period, though, was the triumph of separating sex from emotional attachment.

Also, encounter by encounter, experience by experience, I began both consciously and unconsciously to internalize the positivity of the experiences I was having—to embrace the sense of community from the men I was meeting, even to see so clearly the extraordinary communal love and generosity permeating the whole AIDS epidemic, as amid this incredible plight, men repeatedly volunteered their time, money, and energy to take care of friends as well as strangers, day in, day out, as the prospects became only bleaker. Whatever remnants of stereotypes I managed to maintain really had to give way to the unremitting reality of men surviving despite a plague, men dealing with death in wartime dosages and managing not only to maintain but nurture a really strong sense of a community of love and affirmation. I was surrounded by men who had survived brutal bigotry, been abandoned by their families, faced a peril as looming as the Black Death of the Middle Ages, and still were finding the strength to move on, to accept themselves, and to form new families of their own, as they daily encountered new amendments and roadblocks to their uncharted lives.

Accepting a Homosexual Identity

Creating Families of Choice

In San Francisco, I told my daughter, Alyssa, that I was gay. She was eleven.

It was almost immediately after I arrived, swathed in a state of exaggerated grief from the dissolution of the relationship with John. Alyssa actually had observed that grief firsthand on her visit to Miami, without knowing consciously what we both later believed she probably knew intuitively all along.

During the time I was with John, I had worked very hard to hide the fact that he and I were lovers. Alyssa was spending nearly half of each week with me in New York, but whenever she was to arrive, John would move to a second bedroom, where-upon we would behave like good, heterosexual friends. At the time I felt so guilt-ridden and ashamed of myself and my homosexuality that I hadn't the confidence to approach her honestly and therefore left the truth unsaid.

By the time I arrived in San Francisco, I knew that I could not allow the secret to keep me distant from her any longer. Fortunately, my growing sense of the rightness of what I was doing had begun to overshadow my grief, as well as what I suspect was my fear of losing her. Also, my professional experience both encouraged and nagged me too. I had spent a career in psychotherapy encouraging people to heal and nurture their relationships with the truth, and the results almost always had been positive, sometimes absolutely miraculous. I had two refrains in my head, one nagging at me, saying, "Practice what you preach"; the other encouraged me supportively, saying, "You know the truth will bring you closer together."

Alyssa was living with her mother across the Golden Gate Bridge in Mill Valley. On one of her early visits I took her to a vegetarian restaurant I had discovered. Both of us are vegetarians. With torrents of anxiety I told her I had something important to tell her about myself, something I felt I couldn't keep secret from her any longer. I said I felt it was only fair for me to tell her, for my benefit as well as hers.

We had ordered and were waiting for the food to be delivered. I took a deep breath, and before I could exhale, she said: "You're gay."

"I'm gay," I said, nodding in stunned agreement. "Do you know what that means?"

I wasn't finished enunciating the vowel sound of the word *know*, when I saw her expression change dramatically, as if I had hit a button for a mood switch. Then she began to sob. Just sob. I waited, feeling as if suspended between the last note of the opera and the first hand clap—or moan—of audience response. I waited a long time while she cried, until she finally made an attempt to catch her breath, and I added that I thought she might have known this about me already, that she might have known that the reason I had left the marriage was to deal with this.

"I obviously knew somehow that you were," she said halt-ingly. "And, yes, I know what it means. But putting it into words makes it, like, very real."

Then we both cried, across the table from each other. It was a moment of great tenderness. It did not occur to me right away, but I had put a description on why the marriage had ended, which had to have been confusing for her. We had more or less told her the standard politically correct version—that Mommy and Daddy weren't getting along anymore and had made the decision to live their lives separately; that neither of us were separating from her in any way; that we both loved her and would always be there for her. But this gave her an explanation for the mystery that two par-ents were splitting up who seemingly got along well.

I learned more years later, when Alyssa was interviewed by a teen magazine on the subject of having a gay father. Asked whether she had any regrets about it, she answered that she had one. She was glad that my being gay taught her that she could be whoever she was. It had set an example for her. But she wished I had told her from the start. She said that her father had made a decision to live his life honestly, and yet he did not express that decision honestly to her, and she was most angry about that.

In the weeks and months that followed, my having ex-plained the secret did draw us close and really set the pattern for extraordinary openness. There would be no more secrets be-tween us.

So, whereas I had thought I was going to lose her, I gained a kind of honesty and intimacy that I really never thought I would achieve with my own child. The new, open connection allowed me to keep her very present, even though when I moved back to New York, she was a great geographic distance away. I kept her active not only in my thoughts but in my life, as I developed my new family of choice. She became a central figure, and by choice, because we had developed a genuine relationship based on truth, not on the rules and roles that fathers and daughters were expected to play for each other.

In developing a family of choice, I suppose my initial family connection, my first adopted family member, was my coming-out buddy, Louis, whom I mentioned earlier. We had our inauthentic heterosexual backgrounds in common, our naïveté, and our combined excitement and trepidation about the journey ahead. We shared a great deal together and to this day feel extremely fraternal.

I remember that he also had not talked with his daughter, but more important, he had not talked to his wife about why he had left the marriage. With my encouragement he eventually went to visit her and said, "I think it's time I tell you the reasons why I felt I had this need for independence."

He told her that he was gay, and she laughed. She just burst out laughing, and laughed and laughed and laughed. He stood dumbfounded, lost in a state of embarrassment and humiliation, and finally walked toward the door. As he reached it, she regained some control of herself and said, "No, please don't leave. You're misunderstanding my laughter. Please don't leave." He stopped, puzzled enough to give her the benefit of the doubt, and he returned and sat on the couch, whereupon she took a deep breath, looked up at him, and said, "I'm a lesbian," and then laughed again, until his mind absorbed the idea, first in disbelief, then in irony, then in what he later described as a surprisingly peaceful, knowing acceptance. She said she had been conducting a long-term affair with a woman he merely had assumed was a close girlfriend. He chuckled too.

Now they faced the dilemma of telling their daughter. But now Louis also had a friend, an ex-wife who, as it happened, remained a strong member of his chosen family. He had divorced her, and then he had reconnected with her.

He remained the one important friend whom I thereafter carried through my life, sharing with him a similar process of evolution through our identities as gay men. We kept in contact and visited each other over the years after my return to New York. He remained a brother, and I am in contact with him still.

We marched together in the civil rights demonstration in Washington in the spring of 1993.

About a month after my return to New York from San Francisco, in the summer of 1988, Wendy, a former patient of mine with whom I had become friendly, made a point of saying that she wanted to introduce me to a friend of hers whom she had known from her high school days in the deep South. She knew of my fondness for ballet, and this friend, Joey, was a ballet dancer. Wendy also knew about what had happened between me and John, and having known Joey for a long time, she could attest to his kindness and trustworthiness. She arranged for us to meet by inviting us both to the International Ballet Competition at City Center.

We gathered at her apartment, whereupon—I guess cleverly—she declined to accompany us on the basis of not feeling up to it, leaving the two of us on our own. Upon meeting, both of us felt an immediate chemistry, which I think probably made the situation somewhat tense. We proceeded to this dance event with the awkwardness of any first blind date. Twenty minutes into the competition, two of the competitors from New York were performing a pas de deux, when suddenly her tutu fell to the ground. She had made her entrance onto the stage, and just as she had begun to dance, the tutu drifted lazily to the ground. A look of complete, helpless shock froze on her face. She bent down, picked up the garment, and ran off the stage. Joey and I looked at each other and burst into laughter, and that was the icebreaker.

We then began to see each other regularly. I learned that he was ten years my junior, that he had had a successful ballet career, having danced with several major companies until his progress was severely interrupted and thereafter limited by a serious knee injury. As a result, he was not able to dance full-length ballets and had taken a transitional job as a dancer with the New York City Opera, where he could perform minor roles that didn't exacerbate his injury.

The more I learned about him, the more attached I became.

He was immensely kind and had a sweet manner that was as opposite from John's as anyone could get. I, who was dealing with now deep-rooted issues of mistrust, felt a great comfort and security in his honesty, which as I got to know him better proved to be among his most wonderful assets.

Over time the relationship deepened, and we became a couple, partners in life, and we began to live together. Now performing with the City Opera, he introduced me to a circle of friends whose experiences were very unlike my own. Those who were gay had come out early in their lives, with an ease that seemed to have been tenderly supported by the world of the arts. I found myself completely enjoying their comfort with themselves, and regularly wound up backstage at Lincoln Center, enjoying the camaraderie and the fun of backstage life, with its basis in self-expression and creativity and its periodic release in even more creative, high-camp humor. The language of camp still was pretty unfamiliar to me, and these people employed it as if English were their second language. Whereas camp actually began as a language for gays invisible to one another to recognize each other, its tradition in the theater became magnified, exaggerated, and perfected. It was not a surprise to find someone straight or gay just before a performance pulling costumes off the rack, dressing in drag, and rendering the company weak with laughter as they improvised the customary stage jitters for the entire cast.

A few of the men from that circle began to frequent our home and to attend dinners with us and holiday gatherings— those who were essentially unattached themselves or members of loose circles. As I learned more about them and their struggles and triumphs, I felt more attached, both to individuals and to the ever expanding community.

My association with Joey and his compatriots continued to teach me more and more about creating a family of choice. Just prior to our living together, Joey had been sharing an apartment with an attorney named Arthur in a building on 16th Street, where Joey had lived for ten years, ever since his arrival in New

York. The building was occupied primarily by gay men, and over the course of the years, many of them had lived together in various combinations, as partners, lovers, and roommates. A central corps of men at that address served as Joey's New York family.

Though it was a luxury high-rise, it had the feeling of a gay dormitory. Arthur, for instance, had been a lover to Sam, and after their breakup Sam had moved to the floor above when Joey moved into Arthur's, but they all had remained extremely close friends and attached like family.

This was completely new to me, all the switching that was going on, as well as the changes in status from partner to roommate to neighbor and back, all effected with incredible affection, friendliness, concern, and intimacy. Whatever were the problems between individual people, the communal bond endured.

I was reminded by them that the gay community is incredibly diverse and generous. In that building, there were a few good cooks who would regularly cook for an ad hoc group. Sam, who was less capable in the kitchen, instead offered informed conversation. A banker by profession, he would provide advice for people with growing disposable incomes, while the more nurturing Arthur would provide the meals, and any number of people from the building or from their concentric circles of friends would appear for dinner. They shared in and exuded the same spirit that I found in Joey's southern family, a constant flow of relatives dropping over, calling, gathering together, keeping tabs, visiting in hospitals, borrowing, lending, advising, commiserating, celebrating, and sharing. It all existed on 16th Street.

A small group of the 16th Street crowd, including Sam and Arthur, became members of our extended family. Although many people have moved out of the building now, as their lives improved or as they have gone their separate ways, or, like Sam, have died, still there are periodic gatherings of the clan, from homecomings to testimonials, to memorial services.

I tended to have a more formal relationship with my old

friends, because my old friendships still had some of the formality of my heterosexual life, I guess. My friends tended to be straight, with families and children, and they didn't have the time, the energy, or the freedom to associate casually in the same way that men did who were unconnected by children or by traditional familial responsibilities. I had some very dear friends, like Gillian and Al, who had families of their own, who we went to visit in the way a couple might visit more distant relatives. Because of their own lives, they did not become included in the sort of informal gatherings that regularly happened in our life. We still see them regularly, but as if we are going to visit relatives once or twice a year, occasionally spending a weekend.

I did bring John and his partner, Kal, into our lives—John was a psychiatrist colleague of mine at Ackerman—and they became related to us in this way that was so new to me, although they tended to remain in the outer ring of our concentric circles, probably because they had a well-established life and family of their own. For holidays they often had other obligations.

Various people came and went over the years, and because the people we seem to have collected and been collected by along the way were artists generally—singers, dancers, opera people—they traveled with companies, but they remained in touch while roaming the world, and they gathered with us when they were back in town. The creative life often didn't allow for a lot of time together, but there always seemed to be recurring themes of attachment: postcards from someone singing in Nice, someone else dancing in Spain, or another taking ballet photographs in Paris or Moscow. It continues to this day.

When Sam suggested one summer that we join him and Arthur on Fire Island, we jumped at the chance. I had not had the experience of living in a community that was completely gay, let alone one as singular and beautiful as Fire Island Pines, where residents got around only by strolling narrow, wooden boardwalks lined with bamboo and wildflowers and sheltered from the summer sun by tunnels of scrub oak branches crossing over limbs of pitch pine trees.

When we arrived, we discovered that the house mates who had built this idyllic mist gray house facing Great South Bay were a marital unit consisting of three men who have since become a part of our circle. Two of them had been together twenty-seven years; the third joined them fifteen years later. Together they formed an extremely tight family structure in which they lived together, shared their money, their company, their intellectual and emotional strengths, and shared their lovemaking.

On our first evening, Joey and I—with Sam's minor assistance—prepared a summer feast centered around a grilled swordfish dinner. When the table was set and the meal ready, we summoned the triplets, as we had come to call them, to dinner. They were sitting in the living room at the time. I watched as they made eye contact with one another and then excused themselves, disappearing into their bedroom for a few minutes, while Joey and I wondered if we had insulted them in some way. They came out and carefully chose their seats, and shortly after the dinner began, I asked, "Did we offend you? I mean, when you repaired to the bedroom before, did we say something to offend you?" They laughed and said that, no, they only had conducted a consultation to decide exactly where each of them wanted to sit for dinner.

I marveled at the implications. It was often so difficult for two people to make such a decision. I could scarcely imagine how complicated it would be for three, but they had invented this collaborative system so that they always would present a unified voice and make certain no one would be silently resentful of any perceived conspiracy or slight.

Two seasons later, we're still sharing the house with them.

Alyssa, Joey, and I constitute the absolute nucleus of my family. She was tentative meeting Joey, because she knew that I had been so devastated by my experience with John, but on top of their instantly liking each other, Joey wisely and carefully treated Alyssa with tremendous respect, not trying to fashion a relationship with her but allowing her to decide if she wanted to fashion a relationship with him. Eventually, so much affection existed among the three of us that he was able to be playful and joking with her in a way that either my more serious nature or my role as her father did not permit me to be. Whenever we were together, Joey made it more fun than it would otherwise have been, and Alyssa and I always had fun together in the first place.

When a close friend of Joey's married a Frenchman in Toulouse, we traveled together to attend the wedding, and Joey, Alyssa, and I vacationed for a week on the Riviera. She was fourteen. She has spent Christmas with us, Christmas Eve being my birthday, and for two seasons spent a week with us on Fire Island, once bringing along a girlfriend, and the next year bringing along her boyfriend from California, both of them arriving on the ferry in black leather jackets, much to the delight of the crowd of amused, half-naked gay men meeting their arriving friends and guests at the ferry dock.

In the summer of 1992, while I was on the book tour for *The Patient Who Cured His Therapist*, Joey and I visited Alyssa at one of the California stops. I was signing books and doing readings at A Different Light bookstore in San Francisco and Black Oak Books in Berkeley. Alyssa invited us to meet her at a diner, where she surprised us with a dinner she had arranged in our honor, to introduce, as she put it, her two gay dads to ten of her friends. She had revealed to a few close friends her story about her father, but with our arrival for the book celebration, she "came out" openly to everybody as having two gay dads. We had the best time together, the best.

Contact and association with the gay and lesbian subculture starts to heal some of the developing gay man's damaged self and provides him with the positive images and role models he so desperately needs. He now continues his progress with a subtle change in subjective emphasis and tone, as if he has crossed a line or tipped a weighted scale.

In earlier stages his homosexuality was a central organizing fact of his life, but it was an undesirable fact, and he organized himself around avoiding it, denying it, and concealing it. Now his homosexuality continues to be central, but he has acknowledged and even embraced it, and allowed it to become more a source of positivity and affirmation than of consternation and shame. His positive identification with other gay people, suggests Vivienne Cass, has offered him intriguing if not downright charming answers to the haunting refrains of "Who am I, and where do I belong?" that so plagued him earlier, and he is beginning to surround himself deliberately with reinforcement. This stage marks a new paradigm for his life, in which the reality of a legitimate gay life becomes all-inclusive, and he begins a process of reorienting, in which he eventually winds up rethinking every single aspect of his life as an aspect of a gay life. With each review, each refocusing, he feels varying degrees of relief and freedom, similar if not emotionally identical to the sense of euphoric rediscovery described by people who claim to have been born again with an entirely new focus and/or perspective on life, as saved either by religion, fate, true love, a charismatic cell mate, or a near-death experience.

The new and uplifting perspective also is accompanied by a new and critical view of the dominant society whose prejudices made him feel so miserable in the first place, and his heretofore undirected and covert anger toward it may begin to find enthusiastic expression as he feels the strength of community behind him. Many more subtle insults than before become openly offensive to him, including the most fleeting, nonverbal, homophobic humor and even unconscious displays of insensitivity toward gays and lesbians by homophobic heterosexuals.

But these seemingly hypersensitive feelings serve and strengthen the developing gay man, as his associations during this stage become increasingly—then primarily, and then exclusively, when possible—restricted to gay people who view being gay as fully legitimate and positive in both their private and public lives, according to Cass.

Directing himself more specifically and determinedly toward this sociopolitically exiled community for its support and understanding does tend to highlight and even exacerbate such feelings of separation and distance as he already has long experienced between himself and his heterosexual family. They feel it too, but differently from the way they felt it in the beginning, when their fears of the unknown coupled with their conditioned prejudices were effectively if not overtly rejecting him for his "difference." Now they feel almost as if he were rejecting them for their ignorance.

Of course, he is rejecting them for their ignorance, and although this distancing seems to them to be a highly negative form of maneuvering on his part, it is quite the opposite, and if they had some extra knowledge, courage, and love for him, they would applaud it, for one of the greatest, strongest, and most remarkable adaptive strategies in a gay man's struggle to restore and re-create his life is the creation of a new family. As his healing continues through the acquisition of friends with a deeper empathy, the individual is admired, uplifted, invited to share in experiences that allow him to feel good about himself and admire characteristics in others that he finds reflective of his own. In the process of forming a family, he salves and, over time, heals injuries caused by past disparagements, and he discovers a sense of wholeness and harmony in his new surroundings. He permits himself to reemerge as a separatist of sorts and to form a new network.

Gay men seek to complete themselves and repair their life experiences through the continual creation of a family of choice. The resulting kinship system consists of tremendously diverse relationships collected during the continuous process of coming out. In this stage of the coming-out process, his social identification with gay men helps to shift his self-concept from *homosexual*, the dominant society's name for who and what he is, to *gay man*, a new name, and a new defining category, with its own social rules and cultural knowledge, which he will now begin to learn as a new member. The process involves his accepting his sexuality and also claiming the parts of his character that he repressed or disowned in the earlier stages of denying and rejecting who he was. As their identities solidify, gays continually choose new intimate relationships, friends and lovers, new family members, who in addition to being objects of love or eroticism often serve as temporary familial figures. New family members stand in for old in such a way as to allow members to deal with issues of loyalty, escape from isolation, and arrive at a deeper level of understanding and resolution.

Adaptive Strategies

Creating Families of Choice

For heterosexuals, generally speaking, a supportive family is a given, a safe assumption, a comforting and comfortable condition of life. Gays either cannot depend on their blood ties or legitimately fear that they cannot depend on them. Rare even to the imagination is any implied declaration of intended support for a hypothetical gay member by other members of a traditional family, a message assuring everyone that *if* a member of the family was to one day realize and reveal himself or herself as gay or lesbian, no love for or loyalty toward that person would diminish or be withdrawn.

In the absence of such assurance, the gay family member naturally feels safest assuming that the love and loyalty would change, that disclosure or detection would result in some degree of rejection, pain, and separation.

Because the society is so overwhelmingly homophobic, anti-gay messages permeate most families and then are punctuated in the concentric circles of childhood acquaintants from other families. It does not take long for the gay child to realize that he is different and likely to be ostracized for whatever makes him different.

Moreover, even in the ideal situation—if one exists—in families where a gay member is completely and lovingly accepted, where his sexuality is no more an issue than his height or his hair color, he still is alone among family members with his feelings about who he is and where he fits into the larger society. He has no one in his family of origin who feels quite the way he feels about life, who views the world quite the way he views it.

He knows that, and the knowledge sometimes makes him feel like a living paradox, desperately alone among people who truly love him. He cannot help but know that the other members of his family felt a profound sense of loss upon their discovery of his being gay. His being—who he is—saddens his family. Such sentiment is unmistakably transmitted in the so-called best of circumstances. Even when a family evolves to a process that leads to the acceptance of a gay member, they first work themselves through a process of loss and grief, as does their gay family member.

So, throughout his life the gay man seeks and selects a new family, new concentric circles of family. He chooses the members for what they have in common with one another and with him in contrast to the majority population. One of the most powerful needs they serve for the gay man is in helping him repair the grief and loss he felt when he and his original family realized how separated from each other they would forever be on one profound and intimate level. His being, his very existence, gladdens the members of his chosen family and helps soothe their own feelings of isolation.

Membership in his chosen family is perpetually voluntary, so nobody is a member who does not wish to be. Nor is the gay man bound by biology or genetics to invite the hated pseudo-cousin Ichabod to Christmas dinner. The chosen family often includes members of the family of origin, but it also incorporates lovers, ex-lovers, friends, and children. For support, for understanding, and for connectedness, sometimes for economic stability or for protection, the gay man organizes and establishes the family through love, choice, and creativity. His chosen family exists in contrast to the idea that there is just one form of family that is valuable, and it therefore represents a gigantic act of

creativity in the gay man's departure from the strictures of tradition, the accepted norm, from the life chart passed down
through generations of heterosexual families.

The chosen family also represents the first public betrayal
of the family of origin. Thus it serves paradoxically as a foundation for most future conflicts and dilemmas with that family.

Although the first act of betrayal to the heterosexist family
might be same-sex sexual activity, the major declaration of dis-
loyalty is the gay man's affirmation of sexual identity through
choosing a second family and revealing, usually at some dramatic
point, that members of the selected family are as important, if
not more important, than the blood relatives.

These chosen families do not serve as partial family substitutes in the way that amateur athletic teams, singing sororities,
and fraternal organizations do among heterosexual family mem-
berships. Although psychological support and assistance play a
big part in the existence of chosen families, they also are unique
formations and basically follow previously uncharted courses. A
created family relationship between two gay men cannot possibly
be imitative of the relationship between a blood sibling, because
generally no kinship of homosexuality exists between the brothers, nor is there any way to create an emotional bond between
the siblings on that level. That new relationship must be created
with another gay male in another, unmapped way.

Although the new family is built on a foundation of considerable conflict, it does break away from its more serious origins
and, unbound by conventional rules and roles, becomes increasingly innovative, inventive, and, ultimately, great fun. After all,
whenever people escape or are freed from oppressive and exclu-
sionary rules and regulations, the first item on their agenda usually is a party.

Liberty in the new chosen family takes many forms and
directions. Gay people have an undefined behavioral trajectory.
Nobody in such a family is considered to be abdicating an assumed responsibility or suggesting a departure from any norm,
for instance, if he says that he wants to take over the cooking

responsibilities for a month or two but not be responsible for the aftermath. The deal is struck and can last anywhere from a day to a lifetime, the first rule being that there is no first rule.

Nobody is surprised to see an ex-lover at the door in a gay family, either bearing gifts or introducing his new lover to his former lover, and therefore expanding the family by yet another member. The expectation among heterosexual people is that when lovers break up, they are not likely to see each other again in an intimate situation, certainly not in the presence of new lovers. The opposite often is true among gays. Because they don't couple for the same reasons as heterosexuals in the first place, they feel free to remain attached, somehow, for whatever were the reasons that they coupled in the first place. Relationships among gays are as much about kinship as they are about sexuality, a kinship that cannot be experienced by persons who are not gay.

Jess, a twenty-eight-year-old with a Ph.D. in music composition, grew up just outside Philadelphia, the precocious son of a successful couple. His father was a businessman, his mother a well-known painter. Jess says he felt almost as much loving support from his parents for his homosexuality as for his musical talent, so he cannot be said to have created a family of choice as a substitute for a family of origin that failed him. His family did not fail him. Yet Jess has formed an immediate family of choice whose membership he expects will change as he develops and his life progresses, and, he points out, a second-tier family of gay "first cousins," for whom he feels a less intense but far more lasting kinship.

"My immediate family came together in the same way that one meets someone and just knows that the person could be your next partner," Jess says. "We almost instantly shared a kinship. They're very much my family. There's bickering, not unlike my biological family, and there's a lot of shared support, even financial support. Just recently one of us was having financial problems, and the other members got together about lending him some money. Even though I don't have a partner now, I'm never alone, although sometimes I can talk to them and say I feel lonely. 'I have no friends,' I'll say. Yet there they all are. I think of them as more than friends. I know they're there. I don't have to worry about their friendships, even if I take them for granted, even though I have a supportive biological family. There are a lot of problems I would not go to my biological family to discuss, not even that they wouldn't understand. We just share a similar aesthetic. I have a larger family as well, another concentric circle, a second ring, that includes an ex-lover among others. These are people who don't play a part in my life all that frequently, certainly not on a daily basis, but as an extension. It probably has more longevity than the family I deal with every day. I'm sure the immediate one will change throughout my life, as it has already, but this second circle will always be there, in the way that first cousins are. I can always call them, even after not having spoken to them for a long time, even with a problem. There's a feeling that is different than just seeing old friends, a certain comfort and a warmth, a permanent connection."

The heterosexual family experience revolves around expectations that are unalterably related to procreation, a bonding for the future mixed with loyalty toward the genealogy of the past. Gay family culture challenges accepted cultural constructs that declare that procreation alone constitutes kinship, saying it does not, or that non-biological ties have to at least be patterned after a biological model. They do not. They do not have to be so patterned, gays declare, simply because they don't. Gay chosen families repeatedly prove that they don't.

Gay families have changed the definition of family and continue to change it, literally to suit themselves, and in such armor as they need for their survival in a physically and emotionally hostile world. Theirs is a society that knows no bounds, wherein anything is quite possible, where, as we say, anything can happen and usually does.

However, as previously suggested, if challenging time-worn tenets of family patterns creates support and strength, it creates a powerful and troubling loyalty dilemma as well. The gay man tries to form a family to support him by choosing a family for the loyalty that he might not ever get from his family of origin. In doing so, he immediately becomes disloyal to his family of origin and sets up a life struggle its members can never completely understand, and he can never completely resolve. Worse, the nagging issue of loyalty speaks directly to whatever internalized homophobia still lingers in the gay man's psychological structure. A gay man reared in a heterosexist family cannot have escaped the homophobia contagion entirely. What homophobia he keeps definitely will be stimulated during his struggle with the conflict over his divided family loyalties.

Those divided conflicts get expressed in a variety of ways.

Witty, urbane, professional, accomplished, and unself-consciously gay, Wayne and Barry introduced themselves as close friends for many years, in fact, since undergraduate school. They had lived and worked in cities distant by a traveling time prohibitive to frequent visits and therefore had seen each other only once or twice a year over the past ten, but generally for a week or more at a time. Always when they enjoyed such visits, they capped off days of reminiscing and entertaining with anywhere from playful to passionate sessions of what they thought was purely recreational sex. Looking back on it more recently and from a different perspective, they knew that beneath the laughter and the sensuality, a far more profound relationship had been developing. Eventually they realized that all the while they had been falling in love.

However, beginning with the very moment of that discovery, they became increasingly sexually dysfunctional with each other. As attentive and conscious gay men, they always had thought they had a somewhat superior handle on their sexuality, and they probably did, because gay men often do. But Wayne suddenly became extremely and uncharacteristically demanding in his lovemaking, whereas Barry adopted a passive approach, new to him as well. Each lover was turning the other off for the first time, paradoxically at the very time sex should have been taking on a new and deeper meaning for them.

Perhaps the most painfully difficult reconciliation in the life of a gay male is that relationship between him and his father, whom he loves no less than does any other son, and whose approval he craves no less ardently. Over the years of their acquaintanceship and then friendship, Wayne and Barry had learned the most intimate secrets of what each so loved and feared in his father. Barry's father was a demanding man who expected to be served dutifully by his wife and family. Wayne's father was passive, and Wayne both admired and resented his easy compliance on the one hand and his cowardly acquiescence on the other.

Since they had coupled romantically, Barry and Wayne were behaving sexually in opposite ways from before, but they eventually realized that each man's sexual behavior described how the other's father had behaved throughout their respective childhoods. As if to comfort each other's memories and protect each other's loyalties, the two men had taken on the characteristics of the other's father, self-sacrificially discerning each other's deepest needs and then giving themselves over to serving them. It was beautifully generous but had its consequences: in spirit, each became the other's father. A function of the dilemma of loyalty, it was an impossible situation. The fathers were heterosexual, even homophobic, and opposite to the sons in temperament. The gay man cannot be in bed with his father, first because his father is his father, second because his father is not gay. Actually, the sexual problem Wayne and Barry created appeared to be a way of helping each other maintain his allegiance to his father, even to the degree that it preserved an expression of the fathers' homophobia. They didn't want to betray their fathers, but they loved each other, which amounted to a betrayal of their fathers. So they loved each other without dishonoring their fathers by having unsatisfying sex with each other, solving a grand eternal problem of loyalty by creating a frustrating, immediate one of dysfunction.

Later, and ingeniously, Wayne and Barry created a comedy about themselves and their fathers, a kind of upbeat emotional ritual to exorcise their ghosts and basically get their fathers out of their bed whenever they sense a reemergence of the problem. Their lovemaking thus became theirs.

It is characteristic of an inescapably human process to require balancing sometimes conflicting loyalties to self and family. For gays especially, such balancing involves a titanic struggle for self-acceptance against paradoxical condemnations from known enemies as well as from less obvious sources, among them family members, often well-meaning family members. Wayne and Barry served each other well, maybe perfectly, each behaving in familiar ways, each acting as did the other's father, each serving the other in an effort to deal mutually with issues of loyalty and to repair and resolve conflict. But some conflicts remain conflicts forever, because they have to.

Celebrating
Self-expression

Acting Proud

In the summer of 1987, I decided I was strong enough to return to New York, that I needed to return there. Though I still was reeling from the various states of distress that followed the series of upheavals in my life, from the conscious decision to allow myself my homosexuality to the dissolution of my marriage, to the catastrophic love affair with John and all my consequent misgivings, fears, feelings of loneliness, abandonment, alienation, and self-loathing, I had convinced myself that what I had gained and learned about myself while living in the gay community would support me through any future crisis.

I had developed a growing confidence in myself. I had survived and was surviving some of the worst circumstances a person can expect to endure, including abandonment by a lover—in a way, a first love—who took with him my ambition, my money, and everything familiar to me. I also had survived the move to a new city where I knew nobody and still had managed to succeed both at the new teaching job and as the bereavement therapist, and had endured such extraordinary experiences as I'd had working on the AIDS unit, which on top of everything else was transforming my thinking about what life could mean. I was learning through dying men not only that I was able to grieve for my own comparative losses, but through their boundless courage I was learning the inestimable value of my days, the value of living in the present moment—that old cliché—and also the value of choosing to include people in my life whom I could love and who could love me, because I had seen, over and over, that was what mattered at the end.

I felt fragile but well armed when I decided to leave San Francisco, even though I once again would be leaving my daughter and suffering yet another hardship and loss. But I left because I knew that I was not going to be able to make another life for myself there, despite my attachment to her. The overwhelming reality for me was that San Francisco was a retreat, not my life. I needed to go home to New York, and I needed to be myself, my real self, at home—my real home.

Intuitively I also knew that I was now protected by a growing confidence that would allow me to return and rebuild a life that was based too on courage, honesty, and openness.

I remember, after a sleepless red-eye flight to Kennedy International Airport, climbing the subway stairs to Broadway and 79th, on the upper West Side. It was a hot summer morning. Almost immediately the humidity moistened the skin on my face like a makeup artist, dabbing me with a base coat of blend from the city's varied exhaust systems. I reached hungrily for a lungful of the heavy air, inhaling a tremendous breath in a sigh of relieved, homecoming joy, despite nearly tripping over a homeless man as I reached the top of the stairway.

I was back in my place, in the world-class energy that always had made me feel alive and a documented citizen of the universe. I was simultaneously afraid of this sensation of myself in the process of growing, and not afraid of it at all. I knew that I would be challenged by the daily assaults of New York, and I also knew that I would be meeting the challenges with a new perspective, that of an organism in the middle of a phenomenal growth spurt, ever strengthening, able to withstand disappointments, fight off despondency, and reappear again and again.

After dropping off a package at an old friend's apartment, I was to meet my father on 83rd and Amsterdam and ride with him back to Westbury, Long Island, to stay at my parents' house until I found an apartment in the city. I wondered at the lack of trepidation I felt while scanning the traffic for his face. I felt buoyed by pride in having traveled so far within myself in the past dozen or so months.

We were meeting at crossroads in both our lives. I knew he was worried about me and all of the changes that he had seen me go through—not only worried but completely puzzled by me as well. We had endured a great deal of conflict during my growing up, and he had survived a very difficult life himself.

He was one of three children raised by their mother because their father was absent much of the time. My father always described his as having abandoned the family. I later learned that there was much more to the story than that, but whatever the reasons, my father had basically reared himself on the Lower East Side and eventually found his own way into the fashion industry, without the customary entrees, without the connections, moving literally inch by inch, from pushing racks of clothing through the streets of the garment district to packing boxes, eventually to not only selling women's fashions but actually designing them, sort of. He created a very successful career for himself as a knockoff artist, whose genius was in re-creating from the high couture ideas of elite designers what variations an ordinary middle- and upper-middle-class woman would want to wear. He had a fabulous talent for picking which among the latest designs American women really would want, but he did not have enough talent to design new fashions himself.

All of it had collapsed for him in the seventies, after the top designers realized how much money they could make by selling affordable clothing too. The hallmark of his decline was the explosion in designer jeans, the one trend he bet against. The family who introduced designer jeans to America first proposed the idea to my father to manufacture and sell them. He believed that American women would never accept jeans as fashionable, or even appropriate clothing. He turned them down. They took the idea to Gloria Vanderbilt, and together they made fashion history, and millions.

When I returned to New York, my father, who once had a great deal of pride and who now was feeling a greater deal of regret, was in the process of retiring, selling the house and re-settling in Florida. I was aware, as I waited for him, that he must have been feeling the diametric opposite of what I was feeling. I was returning to New York with this monstrous upheaval behind me; his was yet ahead. While feeling that my whole life had been deconstructed, I also felt that I was reconstructing it again, that the best was ahead of me. I did not regret any of what had happened, and I felt that despite the pain of everything, I was facing the first honest opportunity in my life to fulfill myself.

On the other hand, somewhere in this uptown traffic was my father, more or less deconstructing his life and feeling a fair amount of regret for some bad decisions. For him, business was primary. It was his identity, and things hadn't quite turned out the way he'd expected, the way he had earned every right to expect. His dreams were slipping away. For me, coming to terms with myself was primary; I was within reach of my true identity.

Also, I remember thinking while I stood on that corner that during my year in San Francisco, my parents both had behaved very distantly toward me. While distance was typical for my father, it was very new for my mother. Even for my father, though, this distance was exaggerated. He seemed at least another step removed from me. It was something I could not really understand. I knew all the logical reasons: I had ruptured their dreams for me and consequently challenged their own dream, and I guessed that with moving to Florida and leaving New York, they were dealing with another set of disappointments at the same time. They would not have the amount of money they once had or the wealth they expected to have. They would not have the son they expected to have, either, in the way they expected.

Even considering all of that, the distance between us seemed exaggerated.

We found each other, my father and I, and drove out to Westbury, and I wound up living on Long Island for a couple of weeks, using their house as a base from which to search for an apartment in the city. I thus returned every night to a place that I privately hated, where I had been entombed for so long in my own denial, where I was reminded every morning and evening of all of the emptiness of that young period of my life, from ages nine to seventeen, when I returned to the city to attend college. With the added burden of the feeling of their distance from me, I felt more alone than I should have been able to stand, but at the same time strong and confident enough to stand it anyway, to stand for myself.

During this period, although I was distracted by my search for a new home, I wanted to use the opportunity to bridge the distance between me and my parents. I hoped somehow to get them to shift their view of me from the man I had been to the man I was becoming. In my years as a practicing psychotherapist, I had gained a reputation for being able to show a patient the half of his cup that was filled, to change his perspective, alter the angle from which he viewed himself and permitted others to view him. I wanted to do the same for my parents: yes, their son had followed the traditional map, their map, and, yes, he now had abandoned it, had rejected their way. But look at him now, this son you care so deeply about. Feel his growing pride. Feel for the first time how free he is to be the real son you created and raised.

In a way I wanted to invite them to join me. Here we were in my past, in this house where I had struggled so desperately to not be myself, and now I wanted to find my way back to my parents from that early position, from the beginning of my becoming, and introduce them to the authentic me.

First, though, I found an apartment, on West 84th Street.

Then, one morning at breakfast, while I was preparing to move, I sat down at the kitchen table, the site of all important conversations in our lives, and with considerable fear brought up the subject of their increasing distance over the most recent years, and my sadness and confusion over the possible origins of it. I said with trepidation that I understood that I had gotten off the map, and understood how they might feel disappointed over my having broken up my marriage and especially left my child and my job. I said I wanted them to know, however, that I had not gone through all these experiences because I was gay. I was emphatic. It wasn't that I was gay, I insisted, that I had lost all my money and my place in the world. It was because I had denied being gay for so long that I had to suffer these privations and had to take the most extreme route to my eventual personal freedom. I suffered mainly for all the years I was trying not to be what I was all along.

They didn't appear to understand, or if they did they didn't appear to accept or even believe me; so I took a deep breath and just asked, point-blank: "But why have you been so remote, so far removed from me?"

Eyes cast down, my mother took her time in responding. Finally she said, "I guess we haven't been able to bear the guilt."

"Guilt for what?" I asked pointedly.

"We tried to be the best parents we could," she went on. "I know your dad was very involved in his work life, and absent much of the time. And I was here, of course, doing what mothers do, and perhaps if Dad had been more involved, had taken a greater interest in you, and if I hadn't been so close to you, this never would have happened."

"This? You mean, I wouldn't be gay?"

She bowed her head.

So simple, and I had not focused on it. For the first time

the obvious answer hit me between the eyes: like so many people, my parents not only saw homosexuality in its worst light, as they had been taught, but they also had swallowed the popular translation of psychology's view of its origins, and now they were holding themselves responsible for it, blaming themselves for having failed, for having been bad parents, fervently believing that if they had done something differently, I would have remained heterosexual.

I shook my head. How could they have believed otherwise? How long had it taken me to figure it out, and I was gay? All the information available left them no other avenue of thought. They almost had to believe that something they had done or not done had resulted in my "choosing," I guess consciously or otherwise, to respond romantically to men instead of women.

My father sat silently at the table, clearly in agreement with my mother, as they wrestled with the unfair, impossible, and irrelevant question: Where had they gone wrong?

I took a big deep breath, looked at them, and said, "Mom and Dad, you did not do this. My homosexuality has nothing to do with the way you behaved toward me, although I must admit there was a time that I thought that myself. But now I know, you can't take the guilt for this. You cannot have the guilt for my homosexuality." And then, from my resurrected strength and this sense of growing confidence about myself, I added, "But more important"—I placed my hand firmly on my mother's forearm—"you can't take the credit for it." I repeated myself. "You don't get the credit for this either," I said with pride.

They looked up and, after a brief pause, they laughed. We all laughed. After that moment the mood in our lives seemed to begin to change—not that they were able afterward to accept my homosexuality easily. They weren't. They haven't yet, not completely. But after seeing all my suffering, seeing me now come to them from a position of feeling not only good but proud of myself and my homosexuality changed their whole attitude about me. I think that seeing me in that new light began to release them from their guilt, that reading the pride on my face and even feeling my pride began to free them from guilt, because they couldn't detect anything in me to feel guilty about.

That was the turnaround, the beginning of the new relationship. As time passed, in fits and starts I talked to them more specifically and more extensively about my life, and I told them more about homosexuality in general until they realized that they had believed the popular myths on the subject, even beyond the simple truth that they were not at all responsible. Then, of course, the times seemed to change overnight, and suddenly everyone was talking about homosexuality and gay pride, making my parents' uneasiness easier by the day.

Five years after that breakfast conversation, extremely proud of who I was and of the community to which I belonged, celebrating both myself and the enormous creativity of gay men and also celebrating the publication of *The Patient Who Cured His Therapist*, I telephoned my parents in Florida and told them I was going to appear, live, on *Good Morning America*, and that during it I would be coming out in front of a national television audience. I would be talking about my life as a gay man, I told them, and I wanted them to be prepared for it.

They both were listening, and they followed my announcement with a long moment of silence, before my father said, "Well, you've always been a pioneer." We laughed, if nervously. The next morning, after the show was aired and I returned home to my apartment, I received another phone call from my father. He said simply, "I loved your tie."

The journey from self-acknowledgment to self-acceptance to a genuine, healthy pride in himself combines to create a strength in the developing gay man that helps effect positive changes in the personalities of the society immediately around him, even the heterosexist or homophobic society. People respond positively to genuine confidence. They can't help it. Human beings respect self-respect.

By now the gay man developmentally has progressed from the stage of personal acknowledgment to privately sharing his homosexuality, then to a public presentation of himself that is based on acceptance, honesty, and openness, to where his sexuality has become so integral a part of his daily life, it influences who he is personally, professionally, emotionally, and intellectually. As his identification with the gay community and the gay culture deepens, pride in the accomplishments of the community increases, writes Betty Berzon, and, within the context of now having role models and viewing role models who are successful and fulfilled, and of appreciating a heritage that he perceives now as heroically courageous and noble, he continues to substitute positive views and positions for negative ones at an accelerated rate, some of them subtle, others blatant. He moves from his past experience of withholding the truth about himself, which once had led him to feel powerless, to a new willingness and even eagerness to express openly who he is and what he values. All that once was the reason he felt different, isolated, and out of control about his life now becomes a great source of pride. He is now protected by what he fervently believes is a valid identity. He moves out into the world with less and less ambivalence or defensiveness.

Bolstered by his pioneering membership in a community and culture, he views with a new sense of pride his world and all the identifying hallmarks for which heterosexist people demeaned and diminished it. From inside his community, he looks at behavior he once viewed from the outside as negative and sees it as exceedingly positive. What seemed flamboyant and ostentatious from his old viewpoint, for example, he now sees instead as creative and daring. Deportment that he once condemned along with the heterosexist population as foppish and weak, he now applauds as self-celebrating, exultant, and nonviolent. Men whose company he avoided because they seemed feminine and unmanly he now views as especially sensitive and humane. An acquaintance who dresses in what he once might have ridiculed as outlandish clothing now appears to be boldly reflecting exactly how he feels that day—whether he feels adventurous like a pirate, independent like a cowboy, arrogant like a dandy, or, for that matter, tawdry like a turn-of-the-century madam.

He is now able to envision a life of freedom, happiness, abundance, and honesty in the purest sense of the word.

Adaptive Strategies

Coming Out—Proud

Shielded with this prideful sense of self, the gay man at this stage views the idea of coming out as having an entirely different tone from what he thought earlier and perhaps feared. He now thinks of coming out as unaccompanied by apologies, not hesitant and sheepish, not behaving as if he was peeking out from behind a curtain, but bold and brassy, bursting out exuberantly. He thinks now of his coming out not as an act of anger, defiance, or contempt, but as an act of self-love and of loving other people, wanting others in his life who will love him as he is.

In his enthusiasm, states Berzon, he divides the world for this period into two camps: people who are gay and those who are not. This stage therefore is mined with potential setbacks and disappointments. Every step toward becoming public can represent the possibility of losing an acquaintance or a friend, simply because he is now acting like himself, in extremis, and he had not been before.

By this stage, though, he has survived his worst fears— abandonment, persecution, ridicule, disenfranchisement—and has established exceptional confidence in his ability to negotiate in a larger world that basically hates him. Losing friends at this point only means making room for new ones. It becomes almost retranslated as not losing but jettisoning unworthy friends.

The process of coming out starts with a self-consciousness, in which the gay man begins the passage by telling a few people privately. As he progresses through accepting who he is, through contact with the community, to forming a family of friends, his presentation becomes a public one, in which, with growing pride, he resists hiding who he is. In the process his private and his public self become one.

Dale from Baton Rouge postponed telling his mother that he was gay until he had waded far enough into the process of self-acceptance to have told everybody in his life but her. Finally, when he was thirty-three, he invited his mother to New York for a visit.

A Cajun from a large French Catholic family, she never once had left Baton Rouge after she had moved there as a bride from a tiny Louisiana town. She bore four children, the youngest a hemophiliac who, miraculously, remains HIV-negative to this day, despite the fact that he also is gay.

For years a world-traveling, aggressively athletic ballet dancer who recently had returned to graduate school and earned state certification to teach, Dale had sent for his mother at a time when he was feeling more secure and self-accepting than ever before. Having learned all of what she knew about the major cities of the globe by following his career in his letters and clippings, his mother was openly thrilled about the adventure of visiting him in New York.

On the second day of her visit, Dale bravely sat his mother down in the living room of an apartment he shared with another man. "I was living far away and only seeing my family once a year now," Dale recalled. "Previously I had thought, 'Why tell them? Why hurt them when there's no reason?' I had come out to everybody else in my life. There had been some uncomfortable moments during my visits home when somebody would ask about my life, if I had a girlfriend or when I was going to get married, but somehow, someone in my family always would rescue me with a line like, 'Aw, leave him alone! He's young. He's got plenty of time left to be miserable like the rest of us.' I guess intuitively everyone understood that I would not be getting married. Ironically, when I invited her up, I was well into a partnership I considered permanent, so I felt very married—still do, which is what made it a perfect time for me to want my mother to visit. I was happy and secure.

"And her visit was wonderful, perfect really. So much that I couldn't bear the feeling of hiding something from her. I also sensed that she wanted a deeper connection to me, that somehow she wanted to hear the truth about me. So, that second night, we were having a more than casual conversation about the family, I told her that I loved her and that I had something I had been wanting to tell her for a very long time. I took a deep breath and said, 'Mama, I'm gay.'

"She looked deep into my eyes and said, 'I thought so, baby, but what about your little brother?'

"What about my little brother? I took a double take. Of course I knew my little brother was gay, but it was as if she were saying, 'Baby, I've known that for so long, let's not waste time on it.' I thought I had been keeping this deep secret from her, but it was no deep secret at all, and she had far more pressing matters on her mind. So I said, 'You'll have to ask him.' Which she did. And he told her.

"But when she returned home, she told my father, and soon after, my father called me, and we talked. Basically, without ever using the word *gay*. He reassured me that he loved me, and that was the end of it."

Josh, who previously told us about his first romance, talks about having felt very angry for a while but simultaneously realizing that his anger was not going to get him anywhere. He says he reached a point when he really needed to take action to release the anger. One of the sources of his anger was his having lost the closeness that he had with his family as a child. The simple fact of his being gay had disallowed him the freedom of talking with his family about so much of what was important to him, for fear he might be revealing too much and thus reveal that he was gay.

He was in his late twenties when he decided to stand up to his fears and face his problem, on two fronts. He would write a letter to his parents, telling them the truth about himself, but before he gave it to them, he would tell them personally. Strangely, he said, his anger diminished upon making the decision, and instead of feeling frustrated and frightened, he felt strong and merely nervous. As he composed the letter, he said, his remaining anger began to dissolve into a kind of tenderness and warmth, for his family, for himself, and for this moment in his personal history. He felt as if he were composing a speech for his valedictory address, readying for commencement. He told this story:

"I got on a plane to go home. I knew somewhere in my heart that they were not going to reject me, though I couldn't be sure, and, in fact, I was thinking consciously that if I got thrown out of the house, which I might, that I would live it up for the weekend in San Francisco, where they lived. My mom picked me up at the airport. I had decided beforehand that I would talk with them the next morning.

"When I went downstairs that morning, my parents were sitting in the family room, and I knew I just had to let it happen.

"We had the general catch-up chatter, and somewhere in the general conversation, they said something like, 'We love you.' So I used that as my starting point. I said: 'It's good that you love me, because there's something that I need to tell you that I'm very scared to say.'

"There was deadly silence.

"Then I said, without any hesitation: 'I just have to tell you that I'm gay.'

"Amazingly, my father looked at me and said, 'Well, the first thing we have to do is give you a hug.' And he came over to me and gave me a hug, and he started to cry, and I started to cry, and then my mom joined us, and she gave me a hug, we all hugged and cried for a while. Then I said, 'I have this letter. I wrote it just in case this wasn't going to be the way it worked out. I wanted to leave you something that you could read and maybe understand.'

"I gave them the letter, and they sat there and read it. And they cried again. I never thought that I could be so close to my parents, to really share with them who I was. In my letter I wrote about unconditional love, a phrase that they had tossed about in my childhood, but that I never really believed I was entitled to because I was gay. I guess I believed it was a lie. I explained that I didn't blame them for my believing it. I didn't know who to blame for that, the world, I suppose. I said I believed that they didn't know that they were lying, and that the only way they would find out, and I would find out, would be if they found out who I really was, if they found out I was gay. So I never revealed it because I never believed their love was unconditional.

"But you know, they really weren't lying to me. I learned that from my father's immediate reaction. I felt as if I could have said I was an alien from another planet, or a serial killer, and he would have said, 'Well, the first thing we have to do is give you a hug.'

"I feel so lucky now. I have a pretty close to perfect relationship with my family. My dad is constantly cutting out articles about gay-related things and sending them to me. And my mom is funny. She said to me recently, 'It's fine that you're gay, but you have to meet someone who's Jewish.'

"But I feel guilty too, because so many gay people's experience with their family is so bad. I was really in a good place when I came out to them, and that makes all the difference. I think when you're in a place where you are comfortable with yourself, proud of yourself, you allow for a positive experience to happen. You invite it. If you come from anger, it's much more difficult. This whole thing has turned out to be a gift for me, a gift of communication, that allows the unspoken to be spoken. In fact, pressing my parents to deal with this really emotional experience has opened them up to deal with other issues that they have between themselves."

Advocacy and Activism

The combination of resistance and pride is likely to energize the gay man into action—personal, political, or otherwise—that empowers him. This is an adaptive strategy too, how he converts his anger and pride into something productive. Instead of merely feeling good about himself within the community, he is likely to reject actively those who challenge his freedom, on the one hand, and stand up for his community's rights, on the other. It is at this stage that he holds his lover's hand in public, wears a confrontational T-shirt, marches in a parade, challenges a homophobic comment and just as likely joins an activist group advocating for gay rights or for political and social change, or for a speedier solution to the AIDS epidemic. It is a stage of necessary imbalance, of a cultural jingoism, which he will temper only after he embraces and lives his life as a human being who is entitled to all of the rights and the attendant respect due other human beings.

For the person inclined to activism, in the current climate, there is a megalopolis of avenues for his energy, talent, and passion.

Having been together with his lover, Mark, for four years, and feeling stable and comfortable about who he was, Kirk, an attorney whose activism has both a personal and professional tone to it, slapped a SILENCE = DEATH sticker on his attaché case.

"I had this interview," he said, "for a new job. I had dinner with the key person in the firm and his right-hand man, to lay out what they could offer me and get my response. It was a charming and fun meal, in which everything was going very well. We started to talk about vacations, and I had been saying 'we' this and 'we' that throughout the meal. So the chairman of the department asked me if I was married. Technically, that's an illegal question. You can't ask someone that question in the context of a hiring process, but we were just chatting, like people, so I said, 'No.' Then he asked, 'Oh, a steady?' and I nodded, 'Yes,' and he said, 'Girlfriend, eh?'

"I paused for a second and said to myself, 'I can't let this go past me, and I'm not going to lie.' So I said, 'No, a steady boyfriend.' I felt uncomfortable, nervous. I asked myself, 'Will they hold this against me?' Would it make them think twice, that

I might be HIV-positive and become an insurance problem? All sorts of things were going through my head, but finally I thought, 'Too bad, if this is going to be a problem for them, and I don't get the job, it's probably for the best.' I was glad I put it out on the table. I didn't want to make it clear by putting up Mark's picture in my office, if I got the job."

He got the job.

From his early days working in the criminal justice system, hoping to become the first openly gay warden, to his current impassioned campaign to educate people about violence against gays, Matt, currently executive director of the Lesbian and Gay Anti-Violence Project in New York, has almost always devoted his energies to political action and advocacy. When he was still in law school, he returned to West Virginia, where he had worked for the governor and was something of a political fair-haired boy. There he came out and, as he said, "wore polished nails and an earring in the governor's office. Suddenly I was doing drag shows in West Virginia," he said. "I'd been repressed for so many years, I felt I had to demonstrate that I was gay, and that not to be openly gay was not being true to myself and was a way of reacting to oppression, to being called a sissy, to being called a girl and a fag. I was going to show my father and myself and the world, basically, that I could have the power that anyone else could, that any straight man could. I was always determined to prove that I could and would succeed, that being gay would not stand in my way.

"I no longer feel that I have to prove anything anymore," said Matt, now in his late thirties. "I've accomplished some simple things that leave me feeling satisfied, educating people about violence to gays and lesbians, succeeding at getting the city [New York] to paint the lavender line down Fifth Avenue during Gay Pride Day. I fought for fireworks on Pride Day, and the first time we had them, it was one of the proudest moments of my life. It was emblematic. There was a collective sense of awe. 'We can do this. We can do this. AIDS can kill us, but you're not gonna stop us.' "

MATURING

After the gay man has gained strength, independence, confidence, and pride in himself, mainly through his political, emotional, and social alignment with the sometimes combative gay subculture of the larger community, he can become free to grow beyond the gay-versus-straight mentality (that served him so well) and develop a more realistic view of the society around him and the conditions of his life.

He can accept, for instance, according to Cass and Berzon, that heterosexual people exist who support him, empathize with him, or merely have nothing against him. The fear and anger that fueled his previous stages of development can abate, and he can look at the dominant society as not necessarily universally hostile. He then may also see that gay people exist in his community who have so deeply internalized the stigmatization he has conquered that they can be just as hostile toward him as heterosexists. He now can approach the world more from a position of knowledge and experience than one of fear and avoidance, which allows him to begin the process of integrating his homosexual identity with all other aspects of himself and his life as a full-fledged member of the human race. His personal and public identity in all its complexity can become synthesized into a single self-image, with his homosexual identity no longer given the status he required it to have when he was an emerging gay in a hostile world, but relegated instead to its place among all other aspects of himself, as an integral part of who he is. He can become an adult gay man instead of an emerging gay man, which is not to suggest that he forfeits the continuity of his development, merely that he now may be able to continue to develop in much the same way a man does whose early progress was not so brutally interrupted and sidetracked.

And as he continues to develop, and to age, he eventually rounds corners that lead him into periods of reexamination and reflection. This is part of an ongoing, open-ended process, states John Grace in his paper "Coming Out Alive," that continues throughout a person's lifetime, with the lifelong search for balance and perspective. It involves periodic reevaluation or renewal at numerous points during a life: a taking of inventory, a reexamining of old and new feelings about identity, social networks, old and new relationships, achievements and values placed on them.

From the perspective of a purely chronological life journey, people encounter these benchmarks at such anniversaries as the decades from their date of birth, or anniversaries that are similarly meaningful and temporally spaced. Reaching the ages of thirty, forty, fifty, and sixty thus may inspire this kind of deep reflection and reevaluation. Some milestones are heralded as achievements, others dreaded as periods of life crises, such as mid-life.

A developmental process whose chronology has been so

severely derailed by the dominant society, however, requires the same kinds of pauses for reevaluation and reflection, but they are less predictable and may appear out of order. But with a developing gay man in our society, nearly everything is out of order, anyway.

Reevaluation and
Renewal

Taking Inventory

My own chronological mid-life crisis is what caused or inspired me to return to a crucial stage in my development and start over under a different premise—that I was gay. I reached a point, as an obedient, middle-aged male of my society, when a cursory examination of my life and accomplishments would have resulted in a quite satisfactory judgment of my performance. I would have gotten an A. Socially and professionally I had achieved precisely what I had set out to accomplish. I had followed a legitimate path, accomplished my highest goals and then some, had a successful marriage, a beautiful child, a lovely wife, and was utterly miserable. With a growing awareness of the temporal limitations of my lifetime, I realized that this might be my last chance to honor myself, to be the authentic me before it became too late.

I recognized that while I had accomplished so many of my dreams, I still was an utter failure by my own secret ledger, and I somehow was able to muster whatever courage it took to risk the pain and rejection—and endure much of it too—and effectively start my life over.

But a decade later, at this writing, having journeyed again as a gay man through as many of the developmental stages as I had as a developing straight man, I find myself an adult gay man, having recently confronted the same kind of mid-life-crisis issues I might otherwise have faced ten years ago had my growth not been so interrupted by our society's prejudices.

I have just looked and still am looking at another kind of reevaluation crisis. I spent the decade between the ages of thirty-seven and forty-seven redeveloping as a gay man and now have to face more common, essential issues about life, though with an increased confidence about myself that I suspect comes out of having dealt successfully with the other, more unusual struggle.

Five years into our partnership, Joey and I had developed an established family together and a home. Joey came to grips with his injury and struggled with the acceptance and the re-education required for him to make the transition from ballet dancer to full-time teacher and choreographer. I had reestablished my practice in New York, published *The Patient Who Cured His Therapist*, and ironically been invited back to the Ackerman Institute to help establish the Gay and Lesbian Family Studies Project. I was economically stable again, and both along with and in spite of all the developing changes, our lives appeared to be proceeding rather smoothly.

Except they weren't. While all these aspects of my life were changing positively, there were growing strains in my relationship with Joey. With my greater economic success and increased responsibility, and his preoccupation about restarting his career almost from the bottom up, I saw him as becoming less interested in our household and in his responsibilities to it, and at the same time more distant from me.

The distance began to express itself sexually, with his increasing lack of interest in engaging me. I found myself at forty-four in a relationship in which sex was rapidly diminishing, after having spent an enormous amount of time, energy, struggle, and risk trying to claim my sexuality following a lifetime of repression. It was a natural and almost ordinary development in the progression of a couple's relationship at that time, but my needs were chronologically younger than I, which exacerbated the problem. For Joey, who had come out at fourteen, sex was much more matter-of-fact. He had proceeded quite successfully through the developmental cycles and was considerably more mature than I in his ability to place his sexuality in perspective. I was more mature in another way, having spent my life as a family man knowing how to conduct a partnership. But I was not willing to settle for the remaining part of my life without sex, even without frequent sex.

After some marathon discussions with Joey, I embarked on a series of sexual adventures. I had learned how to separate sex and love, and the affairs I had ranged from one-night stands to sexual friendships that endured over months.

Until I met Peter.

My attraction and affection for Peter was immediate, was absolutely primitive, explosive, visceral, impassioned, and dreamlike, all at the same time—so much so that I still recall that when he first touched me, my mind burst with flashbacks of my childhood daydreams, my adolescent fantasies, the imaginary hands that caressed and comforted me whenever I was lonely and miserable at any stage in my life, including the four days I spent alone and flu-riddled in my last marital home. His were the hands—masculine, strong, yet comforting and sensual. Peter was a baker, and I guess his hands had developed enormous strength from kneading dough, yet also possessed the incredible sensitivity required of a craft that so relies on fingertip, tactile judgment for its artistry.

I was swept away by that, and more.

We began to see each other fairly regularly, and unlike my experiences with previous sexual partners, this quickly be-

came a courtship. Something initially mysterious to me about
how we related to each other, some subtlety in the way he paid
attention to me, even took care of me, was so opposite any experience I'd ever had, I couldn't help but be enthralled, even
breathless.

Both professionally and personally, I had almost always
been in the position of being the caretaker. Peter assumed that
role so quickly and naturally, I suddenly found myself freed from
it, unchained. I gradually realized that his presentation was so
conventionally masculine, it brought out my most feminine side,
which was to some extent a rediscovery of myself. Whereas Joey
captured the side of me that more appreciated the sensitive,
tender, softer, aesthetic, Peter had captured the opposite side of
me, the side that wanted to surrender.

Unexpectedly, I fell in love with Peter, and with who I was
when I was with Peter, and Peter fell in love with me. During
much of our affair I kept Joey informed of the progress of the
relationship. Joey first behaved patiently, but as he sensed my
growing movement away from him, and as Peter's presence became more central in our lives, Joey became more alarmed, then
panicky.

Peter, who had an extremely different background than I,
who had grown up extremely independent, with a good deal of
sexual and social experience in the gay world, had developed a
level of maturity and confidence about himself that was stunning,
appealing. But he had a lot of sidetracks in his life that made
me feel uncertain about a committed partnership with him, although I felt completely committed to him in my love. I was
afraid of his past drinking habits. I was afraid of his abundantly
non-monogamous lifestyle, even though I was being openly non-
monogamous at the time. The intensity of his sexual interest
frightened me, still influenced as I suppose I was—and am—
by heterosexual rules. But whereas John was a wolf in sheep's
clothing, Peter clearly was a wolf, clothed as a wolf and heralded
by a wolf's howl and a wolf's growl.

I still felt somewhat like a lamb.

As the months went on, both men began to press me for a decision about how I was going to conduct the rest of my life, or what I was going to do. Peter recognized that my mind was open to change when I allowed him into my life. He understood my attachment to Joey but chose to react urgently to my disappointments with Joey over the recent year and the imbalance in our relationship. He urged me to leave Joey and convert our partnership into merely a friendship.

Joey, once having refused to discuss our sexual problem and the growing distance between us, now was demanding to discuss it and pressing for us to go to therapy and work out our problems.

In agony, and through a thoroughly awful decision-making process, I reevaluated where I was. I recognized that my attachment to Joey was deep and profound, that he was the first person in my life whom I truly felt I had chosen to attach my authentic gay self to. He was my family, whom I could count on no matter what, and his current behavior was in part a testimony to that —his demand to work things out, his declaration of love, affection, attachment, his willingness to not leave and to see the thing through openly. I recognized the bond. I recognized that the stability of our lives together was important to me, having gone through so many dramatic changes already. And at some deep level I suspected that although I loved Peter, who he was, how he behaved, everything about him, I somehow felt that at the moment, going to him would be more an immediate escape from the troubles I was having than a wise life choice.

Broken-hearted, I told Peter, as I had told him all along, that I loved Joey, that I was attached to Joey, and that I wasn't prepared to leave him now, that I needed to give my relationship with him another opportunity.

Peter cut me out of his life entirely, probably wisely. He told me that my decision would kill his love for me, and he left. I ran into him once, and we did speak briefly. I grieved for his loss for a long time. He remains a very strong memory. He introduced and attached me to part of myself that I would not have known otherwise, and that I can always summon up. Ironically, although I did not surrender to my love for Peter, I learned through my involvement with him how to surrender to a man.

Joey and I have since been repairing our relationship with greater trust and respect, though I must admit that I have greater comfort with the uncertainty of it. I guess the experience of having fallen in love and the occasional yearning for what I had with Peter and didn't have with Joey leaves a smattering of intriguing uncertainty, or an almost exciting lack of reconciliation in my relationship with Joey, despite its very positive qualities, despite the fact that we are simpatico.

Which guarantees that the reexamination process will be ongoing, though I am sure I am reevaluating a different self now, a mature gay self, and for the first time in my life, I can see peace on the horizon.

Generally, when a man arrives at roughly the midpoint in his life, somewhere between the ages of thirty-five and forty-five, he begins to reconsider the choices and the commitments he has made within the context of a changing realization about his mortality and the different perspective he is developing about the passage of time.

Specific choices he has made have absorbed a certain amount of time, and even his relationship with time is new. He feels that he can be more patient—looking five years ahead at a new goal no longer seems so difficult because time seems now to move faster than it did when he was younger—but by the same token, he no longer feels as confident in the amount of time he has ahead of him to accomplish new goals. So he also feels some impatience, especially when he sees the career progress of younger men accelerating by comparison.

This period of high self-examination often leads to a man's deconstructing some elements of his life and realigning them in a rearranged order of importance: what he now thinks he really wants and what he wants to avoid. At some period, and usually this one, every man reinaugurates a quest for authenticity, perhaps one that he feels he abandoned or departed from in a once distracting reach for material satisfaction, praise, or career fulfillment. But the focus and the approach may be vastly different between a gay and straight man during this time of life.

From the outset, the gay man frequently is more prepared for this kind of reevaluation process, because he has been living with it on and off both since childhood and since his earliest acknowledgment of his different sexuality.

Because the gay man was not given the opportunities for participation in institutions like marriage and was forced out of the option to embrace such responsibilities as come with starting a family, he likely developed in his youth an advanced expertise in managing individual freedom and in exploring all the other aspects of life that are not traditionally associated with institutions—nightlife, personal entertainment, socializing, and, frankly, having fun and letting loose. When he reaches a so-called crisis stage, wherein he takes inventory and checks his priorities to see if they still fit, the gay man usually is looking at the possibility of embracing some serious responsibilities. The classic heterosexual man at the same crossroads in life generally is depicted as doing exactly the opposite, as throwing off his too burdensome responsibilities and his career ambitions in order that he may stop to smell the roses, buy a red sportscar, and fall in love with a sexually enthusiastic woman fifteen years his junior.

Reevaluation and reexamination seem to be a period characterized by a fair recognition of the value of love and a strong desire to welcome love as a greater, more dominant ingredient in an individual's life than perhaps it previously had been. Along with the renewed interest in authenticity, the individual becomes more aware of the number and relative proximity of people who love him and with whom he can be loving.

In his more recent relationships, especially after nurturing a lover over the three years prior to the lover's death from AIDS, Hudson was able to transform his own character and expand his definitions of love. A tall, bearded, intense man with a gentle

southern manner draped elegantly over a steel resolve, Hudson
spoke of his reevaluation as if it was a spiritual rebirth.

"Nothing beats transition like death," he said. "Turning
forty was nothing. Breaking up with my last lover was nothing,
except that it restimulated the process of self-evaluation that I
went through with the death of my lover, Mark, two years ago.

"I was thirty-nine when I met Mark. He told me on our
second date that he was HIV-positive. For me, staying with him
wasn't a question. I knew who I was. I didn't know if we would
decide to stay together until the end, since our relationship was
just beginning. But I did know that if we decided to, I would be
there, and that's what happened. I knew who I wanted to be at
that stage of my life. But it was in my experience with Mark that
I created myself more into someone with a deep sense of commitment and honor. This is the way I wanted to live. I have a
strong spiritual belief, which had a lot to do with my decision.
It didn't soften anything. It didn't anesthetize me in any way. All
it did was give me a context, a sense of meaning to the whole
process of what Mark and I were experiencing. In the midst of
all the tragedy, there was a sense of ecstasy as well. We were
experiencing something so transcendent together, so universal,
beyond anything I had ever experienced in the form of love, it
transcended our definition of ourselves.

"We were together for three years.

"It was my choice to break up my current relationship. After
another period of self-examination—this time at forty-four, today
being my birthday—I saw that I was not getting what I needed.
As hard as the choice was, it had to do with being at one with
my own integrity. I was settling. It wasn't for what I was settling
with him, but in myself that I was feeling damaged. I wanted the
experience of unlimited love. He didn't have that capacity. I
wanted to be with someone who was not going to put the brakes
on, someone who was going to go for it all the way. I did it with
Mark, and I want to do it again.

"At the same time I've had this enormous acceleration in
my career over the last two years. Opportunities have been laid

before me that I was not expecting to get in this lifetime. I'm going with them, and I'm creating myself into a person who can achieve what those opportunities are asking from me. I'm suddenly getting a high level of recognition, simultaneously with the demise of my lover. Coping with this level of success seems just as upsetting as coping with the loss and tragedy in some way, and I'm doing both at the same time. There's not much on my plate right now besides self-evaluation.

"Until recently I had a smaller concept of myself. I think anytime you break away from the pack, it gets scary. To break away in the form of success means I have to believe in myself. Even though my being gay might have prompted me unconsciously to mold my self-image into something smaller than what it could have been, it also gave me a great sense of guts and bravery. There's no return to safety when you're gay. I don't think I would have this much belief in myself if I had not spent my life evaluating myself, trying to figure out who I was, trying to justify, to myself as well as to the rest of the world, my right to be here.

"I know I had the guts to go through what I did with Mark and the guts to go for it now. Because it turned out that I was HIV-negative, Mark was to be my experience with AIDS. People were dying all around me and are continuing to. I remember saying to myself, 'Okay, now, here we go . . .'

"It's been a developmental process. I use the analogy of painting, since I'm an artist. First, you rough in everything. Then you start choosing forms and colors and shading and work down and down until things get more and more refined. Eventually you reach the fine touches of the details. The rough being was probably there my whole life. The choices I made coming through had a lot to do with being gay. We are already outside society. As an outsider, I have this opportunity to invent myself, to make my life the way I want it to be. Why not? I have nothing to lose.

"At this point I know I'm not ever going to get to be Hudson again. This is it for Hudson. I want to see what Hudson's got to offer, what he's capable of. I certainly have found roles throughout my life that I'm not interested in, but I know now that I don't want there to be any limits. At forty-four I want to push life as far as I can. It's scary, but so what? This is life, and I want to be out there."

For the heterosexual man, the resurgent interest in love sometimes becomes confused with sex, because he has not attentively separated the differences for himself between love and sex. The stereotypical heterosexual man at this stage of his life can be expected to wind up in a torrid affair with a younger woman, only to discover at some appropriately foolhardy juncture that what he feels is not love but a superficial passion that reminds him of his youth and both temporarily blocks and then permanently punctuates its long-ignored terminus. Unseparated sex for the straight man is deceptive and takes on the trappings of true love and commitment. Then it falls apart, because it was just sex.

That confusion seems to be much less of a danger for gay men, because they already have learned to separate sex and love in their lives to the degree that some sex has absolutely no relationship whatsoever with love but is merely recreational. Having made that separation, gays tend to be much more sensible in selecting partners for truly mutually supportive emotional relationships.

Interestingly, in this day and age that heterosexual man in mid-life crisis may be stopped short by a fear to which he had not devoted much time or thought, at least not if he has heretofore been monogamously faithful: the possibility of contracting AIDS. His gay counterpart, on the other hand, cannot think of sex without also thinking of AIDS.

For similar reasons, whereas the heterosexual man between thirty-five and forty-five may be reviewing his life inspired mainly by his first healthy meditation on the inexorably approaching end of it, the gay reevaluator has been staring at the likelihood of his own death for all the years that his friends and neighbors have been prematurely dying around him. He has been living as if in a war zone, and for him mortality is no abstract concept. It is an ever present element of life that causes daily stress and trauma, raising new doubts every time he encounters new acquaintances or risks new friendships.

AIDS has forced gays to deal more intently with the concepts of present and future and to rebalance the idea of what time they have left and how they should use it, because so many of their friends are dying or living with the dying.

AIDS, in fact, has created an all but missing generation of gay men. My chronological peers, men in their forties, many of them the pioneers of gay liberation, are missing, wherever I go. If I visit predominantly gay enclaves like the vacation community of Fire Island Pines, on the south shore of Long Island, I am ever conscious of the abundant population of gay men in their twenties, thirties, and sixties, and the relative absence of my contemporaries. Where are they?

They are dead.

For those who have survived and who are HIV-negative, an unusual immediacy about life has pressed many of them into what more customarily would be a later-in-life reevaluation at a much earlier chronological stage, accelerating that process of reviewing and renewing, forcing them to measure the remaining estimated time and try to figure out what they most want to do with it.

But because gay men always have lived with uncertainty, as well as a creativity fostered by life outside the charted course, they tend to be almost prepared for the unexpected, and the confrontation with self-inventory does not shock them as severely as it tends to shock a straight person.

The process of reevaluation happens in stages, beginning with the individual's feeling that he is stalled or that time has stopped for him. The catalyst could be that a physiological limitation has reared its ugly head for the first time, or that a younger colleague-competitor has reared his, but the resultant feeling almost always is that the individual is stuck, trapped, not moving.

Upon reflection, a smart individual invariably concludes the simple truth that he is responsible for his own life, and basically alone in that, which is to say, solely responsible. Whatever is working, whatever has failed, wherever he has or has not arrived, is a direct result of such maneuvers and decisions that only he has made, nobody else. He is alone with his life, and he recognizes it.

Next, he reevaluates his life dreams, faces up to his image of himself, the one that he had earlier in his life and one that his imagination is putting together now. The dominant dream may be professional, wherein he views his place on the ladder of his own expectations and then those of his family, friends, acquaintances, and competitors; it may be social, wherein he reviews his status as a man with or without a mate or a society he deems appropriate to him; it may be paternal, wherein he reevaluates either his performance as a father or his decision to become or not become one.

The heterosexual man arriving on time at this juncture may find this alone-ness a moment of profound recognition, because for as long as he has not been paying this kind of attention to his progress, he has been comfortably aware of grand concentric circles of supportive systems around him—his immediate family, his extended family, his neighborhood and friends, his community and its structures, his government and his religion, his society and its history and the history of societies before it. He also is aware of such pressure as the members of these societies, communities, categories, and groups place upon him to be responsible to them, accountable and answerable to them, for his support, for his performances, and for his behavior. So the heterosexual man frequently faces the questions of how good he has or has not been to himself and how much enjoyment of his life he may have abdicated in the name of responsibility and how deserving he might be of the stereotypical trappings of a classic irresponsible mid-life freak-out.

The gay man, however, is a little more prepared for the realization that he is fundamentally alone, because he has been realizing it for some time now. He already has passed through great chasms in his life, sometimes with nobody nearby whom he could count on, nobody whom he could trust. He has depended on his own resources. He knows he has created his present and is creating his future under whatever difficult circumstances he encounters. He has developed the talent and skills for living independently, and therefore, at this point, for him the debate is likely to be the opposite of the heterosexual man's.

His debate may be about whether he is prepared to surrender some of this independence and develop more permanent attachments and more conventional responsibilities. If he has been long partnered, he may be reexamining the option of living without a partner. He may, on the other hand, be reevaluating his freedom and lack of permanent attachment, determining if he needs to experience a deeper kind of commitment, such as that to a permanent partner or to a child as a parent.

Each entrant to this stage finds himself reevaluating the roles he has played, which among them have felt right and which disappointing. The straight man is likely to have played the roles of husband and father and is liable to feel boxed in by those roles, enjoying them to some degree but being disappointed in himself and in the other players as well, perhaps not feeling appreciated for some of what he has done or the security his efforts have created. The gay man, who has challenged stereotypes and who probably has had enormous flexibility in his life playing numerous roles, sexually and otherwise, has been free from such confinement and has been changing throughout his life thus far; so the struggle for him is not a question of a dramatic reevaluation of roles as much as it is a curiosity about exploring the more permanent roles he has not played, including conventional life roles he has avoided or were forbidden to him, like becoming a father.

The question for the heterosexual man is what he has gained by belonging so much to his society and whether he wishes to continue belonging to the same degree. The question for the gay man is the opposite: whether he is tired of being a desperado, shielded from further disappointment and rejection by his careful solitude, and wishes now to risk belonging to some larger society, from a couple, to a group, to a community.

As the period of reevaluation and reexamination draws nearer its denouement, the individual passing successfully through it experiences a refreshing sense of renewal and recommitment to life that gives him a reason to look to the future with excitement and hope instead of stagnation and dread, whether the choices he faces revolve around his satisfaction with himself or with the various roles he either plays or wishes to play: a productive contributor to the community, a wise and loving father, a worthy life partner, or a proud and solitary man. All are potential adaptations to whatever he concludes as he emerges from his own reevaluation. They are all possible strategies for adapting to his new resolutions, choices open to his selection and development, courses upon which he may chart the rest of his life.

Adaptive Strategies

Fathering

By the time a gay man reaches this stage, the major choices beyond those regarding his occupational ambitions are about coupling and procreation—does he want to commit himself (or stay committed) to a traditional partner, or be on his own, and does he want to become, if he has not already, a father.

As increasing enlightenment about homosexuality affects younger generations of gays, fewer men will arrive at this stage of life as I did, having already become fathers by first being married. We probably always will exist, however, to the extent that the numerical minority of the gay population always will inspire the kind of fear and suspicion that percolates into hatred and ostracism, which in turn results in gay youths trying to grow against their nature into heterosexual adults.

That path, so common among my rapidly disappearing generation of gay men, adds an odd wrinkle to this stage of life we are calling reevaluation and renewal, in that those men go through the entire process twice, as I did. First, while they are strenuously masquerading as heterosexual men, the so-called mid-life crisis serves as a launching pad for laying aside the conventional chart and coming to terms with their homosexuality. Then, as homosexual men who in their non-chronological, bumper-car way have passed through the stages of development that bring them to gay adulthood, they now face reevaluating themselves again, but as mid-life gay men.

That can make them a pretty complex group. Among them are some individuals who do not acknowledge their homosexuality until after their marriage, and some who enter marriage fully aware of their homosexuality. I fell somewhere in between even those, as a gay man episodically aware of his homosexuality but involuntarily denying it most of the time, and then forgetting the episodes entirely.

In the case of the men who knowingly marry despite their homosexuality, some are merely trying to conceal their truth; some have a genuine affection for their female spouse and a desperate longing to be what their surrounding society expects them to be; some are terrified of loneliness; and many have, as many openly gay men quite naturally have, a genuine desire to have and raise children. The complicity of the spouses in these unions vary similarly, for only some gay men conceal their sexuality so brilliantly from themselves and from others that loved ones are perfectly fooled. Most others cannot and do not create a perfect charade, and the women who marry them must contribute to the conspiracy (according to M. S. Hatterer, writing in the *American Journal of Psychiatry* in 1974, whose studies suggested that women married to gay men ignore the signals about their spouses' homosexuality as a way of staying in a relationship that meets their needs).

Nonetheless, making the decision to move out of such a marriage and into an openly gay identity tends not to be a straightforward negotiation but an involved process that sometimes requires "moving back and forth, in and out of the so-called closet," writes G. Greer and F. Bozett in their article "Lesbian Mothers and Gay Fathers," reaching different levels of pain, dissatisfaction, despondency on the one hand and desire, hope, and courage on the other. Each level seems to be achieved by a painful searching process wherein the individual struggles to negotiate with the larger world in his different and seemingly mutually exclusive roles as husband, father, and gay man. Complicating the process is the extent to which he and his wife truly love each other. She no doubt will suffer feelings of anger and betrayal beyond what she might ever have feared, given that the idea of divorce alone might have been unthinkable. Now she contends with the possibility of years of duplicity, while he wrestles with both her pain and the guilt he feels for fooling or having tried to fool both of them. Factors above and beyond the personal and economic agony in dissembling a marriage appear to be designed to make the negotiating even more difficult, including deciding the question of whether the gay world will offer any greater support than the straight world to a homosexual man with parental responsibilities.

Probably because parenting was simply not a part of the manifest gay culture historically, the culture tended to be much more oriented toward the individual and individual freedom, with people having fewer long-term commitments and fewer financial obligations. Gays collectively placed more emphasis on personal freedom and autonomy and probably looked down upon the idea of having followed a heterosexist map. The gay father comes to this culture with a lot of emotional and financial restrictions that lifelong gays are not accustomed to, and it is not uncommon for gay fathers to tell me that because of this they have experienced a certain amount of discrimination and rejection from gays who are not fathers.

Moreover, the gay father who has been in a long-term heterosexual marriage tends to attempt initially to find a similarly long-term gay relationship, precisely what he does not need while faced with the amount of unlearning he has to do as part of his developing through such stages as we described earlier. He still is inclined to cling to the enormous experience as a heterosexual having chosen that life either out of fear, uncertainty, or in an attempt to force a structure on himself that would keep his authentic gay self from arising, as he has long feared.

In their book *Gay Fathers*, Robert Barret and Bryan Robinson report that the acceptance of both identities in both worlds, being a gay man and father, allows him to incorporate a positive image and confirm his two identities as compatible and acceptable, but that change occurs over time. The degree to which the father accepts his homosexuality and to whom he discloses it parallels how he is going to disclose himself in the gay world as a man who has lived as a heterosexual family man. There is no reason why he cannot be both gay and a father and naturally assume his place in both worlds, except that he has been conditioned to believe otherwise.

Increasingly gay men who have lived their adult lives as gay have been moving toward siring and raising children outside of traditional marriages, and thus have been creating new definitions of family and family life—this in a non-traditional culture of which children have not been part. For the contemporary gay man, the notion of having children is at least as desirable an ambition as serving in the government, teaching theology, or piloting a spacecraft.

However, it is equally complicated.

The biological imperative to procreate and nurture does not discriminate based on race, creed, national origin, or sexuality. It is as human as hunger and thus strikes all members of the species at one time or another, in one degree or another. Furthermore, in the cultural climate of the AIDS epidemic and the new social structure emerging from the gay community's response to it, nobody should be surprised if the community's desire, collectively and individually, is accentuated to nurture, mentor, or actually produce children, to have an historical connection not only to ancestors but to descendants. Liken it to a childless woman between thirty and forty who feels her biological clock ticking; this is an entire culture whose biological time bomb is ticking.

But the prevailing view of the predominantly heterosexist society is that an aspiring gay father is repulsive, condemned to cause irreparable harm to any of his issue because of his aberrant sexuality. Not only does the society reject his presumption to human normalcy by its unwritten prejudices, it rejects institutionally such applications as he might dare offer it toward his ambitions for fatherhood. It cannot stop him, but its intransigence heralds its future behavior toward him and his children and is one serious element he must consider in his deliberations on going ahead with whatever plans he has concocted.

The plans are likely to be imaginative too, as gay men in appreciable numbers already have combined reproductive forces with lesbian women to produce children and raise them under creative variations of joint physical and legal custody, as if the children were the issue of an unusually friendly, mutually respectful, and distantly affectionate divorce. In few of the cases does the gay man choose a stranger with whom he will have a child. The mother generally is a friend, and that seems to be the predominating factor in making the decision both happen and work. He may choose to co-parent with a lesbian couple who have a similar desire and with whom he has had a long-term relationship. The friendship shifts into a co-parenting agreement. We do not have enough experience with it as a social phenomenon to know, but it does not take an especially fertile imagination to conjure the potential difficulties. With no romantic attachment, the arrangement can become on the worst end like a bad divorce, on the best, like neighbors and friends who call each other by endearing, fictitious family names like "Aunt" and "Uncle."

Those fictitious names themselves are less likely to surface in a gay family, however. The fluidity of changing relationships among gays and the possible social permutations unfettered by the sanction of legal marital contracts always implies that "Uncle" Bob may not be Dad's lover next year. With AIDS—always there is AIDS—he may in fact be "the late Bob" by next year, so we'll just call him Bob.

Moving a lover into and out of a gay family in which there is a child is bound to present emotional complications that sociologists haven't even begun to explore, but it is safe to say that the very idea suggests formidable challenges. Men who come into the gay world as fathers already face including a lover in their lives and identifying him to their children. In many ways the new gay family may resemble the heterosexual stepfamily. The possibilities for complications are legion and so wide-ranging as to include two men coming together as lovers, both of whom began their adult lives as heterosexual mates and both of whom are fathers, but it is more likely that the gay counterpart to a stepfather will have little or no experience as a parent and probably will have heretofore lived free of such responsibilities as parenthood presents.

Sharing a lover's time with his child is bound to lead to some conflict; attempts on the part of a non-parent to understand the strength of a bond between a father and his child sometimes falls short, and the relationship between the adults and between the father and his child is likely to be affected.

Despite the complexities, gays not only are recognizing their ability but their right to bear and raise children, as equal to their rights to life, and liberty, and such pursuits as fulfill them and make them happy. If overcoming more than the average number and size of obstacles is part of the package, the imbalance is not unfamiliar to them, especially to those whose most difficult challenges already are behind them.

Michael is a contemporary gay father of a two-year-old daughter who lives under the primary custodial care of her two lesbian mothers. An attorney, he had known one of the women, Lucy, for the four years she was his boss at a law firm in New York. On a visit to New York from her new home in Jackson,

Mississippi, Lucy mentioned that she and her new lover were planning on having a child. In expressing both his delight and envy, Michael made an offhand comment that he would like to do that sometime, and that he was sorry she lived so far away, because she would be a wonderful person to be involved with in that kind of . . . project.

"She called back a few weeks later," said Michael, "and asked how serious I was and then told me that the man they had planned to have as the father had decided to back out. I went down and met Lucy's lover, Susan, for the first time, over a weekend, where we were sort of feeling each other out in a sort of courtship kind of thing. We talked through the weekend, and I got to know Susan very well. We talked through what we thought all the difficult issues would be, included among them what role I would play in the child's life. I think they were attracted by the geographic distance, while I was put off by it, although I certainly didn't want to be the custodial parent. I didn't know what they envisioned telling the child about me, until it became clear that they envisioned having a man who was known to the child as a father and who was incorporated as an important part of the child's life, but who would not be there every evening to say good night and every morning to say good morning, who would be a continual presence, but not physically, in the child's life.

"We talked about religion—they're both Jewish, and I'm not—and how our respective families would feel about a child being brought up in this constellation of parents, how we would incorporate them into the child's life. Because Lucy and I are lawyers, the result of the weekend was that we went back and thought about it and had a series of phone calls.

"We decided to go ahead and do it, try to impregnate Lucy. We also decided that we would have a written document that would embody our agreement. The agreement was thirteen pages long.

"I wanted to have a biological and emotional relationship to a child. I wanted be a father, and it wasn't the kind of decision that would foreclose on my being a custodial father sometime in the future, if my life developed so that was possible. I was in my early thirties. I was not in a committed relationship with a man, and I was feeling that I did not want to put anything on hold anymore. I wanted to make a compromise and do what was possible rather than hold off for something that was perhaps more perfect or ideal. I knew that if I was going to enter into this kind of agreement with a lesbian couple who lived on the upper West Side or in Park Slope, it would be very difficult for me not to call all the time or not to drop by and not to have hurt feelings when I wasn't welcome. Here, with the distance, I wouldn't be putting myself in situations where I wasn't welcome. I loved their home, and their relationship seemed really honest and good. The child would be a happy part of their lives and would be well loved.

"I definitely felt like I was at the top of a roller coaster and sort of going down and letting go and doing it. Lucy and I, in our little document, tried to control out all the contingencies. We both realized—all three of us realized—it was impossible for us to control. It was going to be out of control. That was part of the attraction in it too.

"Very rarely did friends approve of the idea. My family was never disapproving, but they were slow to become excited. Once there was a pregnancy, a fetus that had become a child, the excitement grew, and so did the support. Both Lucy's family and my family became excited, and pretty soon there were squabbles about the name and what last name the child would bear. It seemed like the right decision to have the non-biological partner's last name be the child's, as a symbol to the outside world that she was a parent, not a friend but a parent. In fact, she is the primary caretaker to the child, because she is the mommy. Her family was slower to get excited, but since Anna was born, all three families have been completely charmed and delighted and supportive.

"When we were doing the impregnation, there was a lot of physical intimacy. Although we didn't have sex together, we were both having sex independently. I started dating Bob then. We had sex together and I came into a cup, and we passed it to them, and they went into the room, and they had sex together, made love, while they were doing the insemination. Then the four of us hung out. It was like the afterglow feeling together. We talked about what we were doing and hung out.

"I had related to my employer what I was going to be doing, so when Lucy went into labor, I was packed and ready. Literally within hours I was in Jackson. It was a long labor, something like twenty hours. I was awestruck in the delivery room. The feeling of having Anna in my arms for the first time was very spiritual. And from that point on, I started coming down every four or five weeks, the first year. During that time, for the first time, I started to feel that I had made a mistake maybe—that I was not going to be emotionally satisfied by the distance of the relationship. I kept waiting for a glimmer of recognition in Anna's eyes or in her conduct. I could have been the mailman, though, and that hurt. I think I felt a little panic-stricken that it was the wrong thing to do, and that all the people who had told me I was making a mistake were right.

"After the first birthday, we had some couples counseling. It's not all settled, but we went to the therapy sessions and talked about it and the frequency of my visits, and we reached an understanding. At that point I was insecure about whether the intense emotional feelings I had toward Anna would be returned by her. I didn't want to give up anything in terms of frequency of contact, because I thought that would make this emotional contact less likely to develop. We agreed that the purpose of my visits would be to make sure that this emotional connection could be nourished and grow while understanding that the purpose was not to interfere with the rest of their life. I would have to be flexible and accommodating to the rest of their needs.

"As far as being a father, the bond that I was worried about has very definitely formed. My insecurity about that has just dropped by the wayside. Before Anna was talking, she started to show recognition for me in simple things—like when I would hold her, she would always play with the hair on my chest in the same way. She would remember little games we had developed together. She knows that Daddy is interested in certain of her toys because we've played with them before, so she'll bring out the toy that we played with the last time. Since she began talking, any last vestige of insecurity has dropped away, because her eyes light up when she sees me. She says, 'Daddy,' she comes to me, she wants to hug me the first thing off. She wants to show me whatever is new in her life.

"I feel a sense of excitement and well-being when I think of her. It feels like the beginning of a new relationship. You know how it's fun when you're first meeting someone and there is always enormous possibility? That's what it feels like to me and has for two solid years, and I feel like with every year, it will feel the same way. I'm just excited about being part of her life and being with her as she grows.

"I feel very much like I did the right thing. It has been a source of anxiety, but I'm just so excited by her. It's kind of liberating. It's paradoxical. The way that I interpret the father's role in being a parent is very confining, and the way that it is for a custodial parent is certainly confining, but for me, I feel liberated by it. I feel like there will be an outlet for a kind of love and emotional connection that I want to have with a child, which I can do without having any of the baggage. I think the kinds of resentments that grow up inside a family, with your parent, I think I probably will escape them. I'm just delighted by things that annoy her mothers, for instance. She's in her two's, and she can get tantrum-like, and I can see that it is a battle of the wills, and I feel completely outside of it. I think it's just delightful."

Ongoing Relationships

The stage of reevaluation and renewal at any age and for either sexuality can be particularly threatening or invigorating to an ongoing, emotion-based relationship, even more readily between gay lovers than between husband and wife.

Among contemporary gays, a mid-life issue or sometimes a medical crisis like an HIV-positive diagnosis will precipitate the reevaluation. But many gay men reach the point of reevaluation without ever having been involved in an ongoing relationship, because they now are considering one as a result of their reexamination of their lives.

Reevaluation is inevitable for people who have aligned themselves with another. All couples periodically question their commitment to their commitment, generally during a slump in their relationship or after a collision of needs and expectations that strikes both partners as a disappointment. The same reexamination that raises the question of commitment also serves as an opportunity for the participants to create new meaning and purpose in their individual lives and then together as a couple. The dreams that may have served them both well in the early part of their relationship may not have the same import anymore and may not therefore be able to carry them over to the next stage. For couples who have developed a stable and loyal attachment, passing through the stage of reevaluation will either create new significance or the relationship will become stunted, as will the individual members, and it will dissolve.

In a gay relationship, dissolution is more of an option, and not as cumbersome to effect. Less outside pressure exists to perpetuate the union, such as that created by the government-sanctioned, religiously liturgized institution of marriage. Gays have no such outside pressure to keep them together. Each partner asks at this stage what the relationship has provided for him, both in terms of how it has encouraged or inhibited him and in terms of what opportunities it has offered him to be generous and loyal, to give as well as to receive.

Whatever issues have not been resolved in the relationship but maybe simply managed now become primary targets either for resolution or as pivot points for dissolution, weighed down or buoyed by issues that are perfectly natural and common to this stage, including disappointment in the self and in unrealized dreams. One man may have succeeded professionally in a way the other has not. One may be aging well, maintaining his physical and therefore sexual attractiveness, while the other may not, giving rise to new jealousies and a competitiveness that was not always a part of the relationship. A partner who spent much of the relationship playing the role of caretaker may be arriving at the conclusion that the duties ought to be more equally shared, or that he does not want the responsibility at all anymore. He may feel tired and disillusioned and may be wanting to be taken care of in a way that he has not allowed himself. Yet the structure of the relationship may not have allowed for that kind of flexibility.

Gerard and Stephen, two of my summer neighbors at Fire Island Pines, talked freely about having passed through the re-examination stage, and I recorded their conversation. Gerard, thirty-nine, and Stephen, thirty-five, had been a couple for fifteen years.

STEPHEN: Gerard and all of the carbon copies of Gerard in my life represented my opposites. I was the choirboy. The responsible one. The older son. The best boy. When everyone played all summer, I worked in my father's service station. In college, my friends were having a gay old time, out dancing all night, taking drugs, while I worked. I acquired the choirboy persona as a mask to hide behind. Certainly the responsible son thing was laid on me early on. But at the same time, I figured that's what I had to do to be accepted. And if I didn't, they would find out the truth about me, that I was gay, and I would be cast out.

GERARD: Stephen represented an escape from my family and my environment. His stability was something I never had. [To STE-PHEN] You have been and still are the anchor in my life.

STEPHEN: We were drawn to the opposites in our natures, yet we both resisted taking on these qualities in ourselves that we so admired in the other person. It's only now, after learning that I have HIV, and in re-prioritizing my life, that I've really allowed myself to loosen up and be what, or explore what, I've always wanted to explore. I fought it for many years, which brings us to the crisis of two years ago.

It was a year into my diagnosis. At first I had myself a good cry for a few weeks after I found out, and then I decided everything was fine and I'd just continue with my life as is. About a year later, Gerard and I moved, and I felt railroaded into the place that we were getting. Everything was making me irritable, including that I had just started on AZT, which does in fact make some people irritable. I began to rebel against the responsibility of the relationship, against having been depended on for everything. I had already been getting tired of that, and then on top of it, finding out that I've got this virus, and waking up one day and thinking, "Who knows how much longer I have? What have I done with my life? What have I missed?"

I realized I had been the responsible goody-two-shoes for thirtysomething years. I'd been in this relationship with Gerard for twelve years, and I thought, "What have I missed because of it?" I wondered about all of the things that I had not experienced but that Gerard had—all of the fast-lane living, not having to worry about anybody else, doing and going as I pleased, not being tied down to anything or anyone.

Here I was, faced with this potentially terminal illness, and all I could think about was my imminent death, proceeded by a lengthy, disgusting illness. I thought, "I don't have time. I have to find out."

Had I left Gerard then, as I fantasized, I would have probably gone straight into the arms of Dan, the other man in the picture, and probably been very quickly disenchanted with that. When I weighed all the options, made up the pro and con lists in my mind, I think there were slightly more pros to staying in the relationship, looking at it as dispassionately as possible. This thing called love kept getting in the way. No matter what lists I came up with, that wrenching feeling that I could not leave him kept coming up. Somehow I knew that I could not be whole without him. All of this had not resulted in the diminishment of my love for him. It hadn't burned out, spent itself.

GERARD: Even though I had been sober five years by then, I still had no idea how to deal with my life. My life had always been handled by Stephen. Learning that Stephen was HIV-positive, I discovered that there is a part of my personality that wants to take care of someone. I was really going to be there for Stephen. I knew being a recovering alcoholic, having gone through that, I would get through this. This would be just another challenge in my life. It didn't traumatize me. If anything, it gave me a chance to do a rescue mission.

STEPHEN: Gerard didn't remain static during all of this. He was making extraordinary concessions and allowances. Gerard was adapting and changing, primarily in the sphere of taking responsibility, taking equal share in the relationship. I think we've each come more to the center now. At first we were diametrically opposed. We're both more equal parts, wild and stable. We haven't switched roles entirely. It's not in our nature to do that. But we have reached a middle ground.

GERARD: These three years have been amazing. I don't think we could get any closer than Stephen and I have gotten. This crisis made us confront the responsibility of what a relationship is. I was never confronted so bluntly with the fact that there was a chance I could have little time left. I had a vision of a new life, a new beginning.

STEPHEN: That has been the major benefit. It's to be able to say this: it's what I need, what I want. It's only possible now because Gerard can hear that and not be threatened by it. He's no longer threatened by us acting as individuals, having a certain amount of independence. And that's the new beginning.

In other cases, explains Betty Berzon, the vestiges of prior developmental issues reemerge, epilogues of conflicts that either partner has not completely resolved. For instance, the partners may be at different levels of coming out—one partner cautious and private, the other having publicly presented himself. That partner may have worked through cultural norms and values of heterosexual family life in such a way that he has enormous flexibility in his ability to enact gender roles, while the other may not have progressed and be more tied to the conventional male-oriented roles with which he was raised. Regarding the issue of intimacy, one partner may have not thoroughly worked through his internalized homophobia and therefore may have constructed subtle barriers that inhibit his ability to be intimate in a continuous and committed way, while his partner may have evolved through that issue quite satisfactorily.

According to Berzon, examples of relationship problems resulting from developmental differences exist abundantly. A partner may have acknowledged, assumed, and accepted his homosexuality, but may not have had very positive experiences in the gay and lesbian community. He may have isolated himself and devalued the gay community at large, mixing in elements of his own self-rejection and projecting it onto the gay community, while remaining in a relationship with a man who has a much more successful experience within the community. He may have been content for a long time because of the romanticism of their relationship, but now may be yearning for connections within the community while becoming weary of his partner's negativity.

People seem always to return to whatever they have left unresolved in even the earliest stages of development. Despite a strong attraction for each other and a seeming compatibility in early years, an adaptive strategy that one partner used in those years may now interfere with the successful continuation of the relationship. For example, frequently a gay man denies his erotic attraction at an early age, and while he is able to essentially move past that effectively, at least enough to have sexual relations with men, his ability to be free-spirited about sex may be curtailed. As time goes on and the initial excitement of a lasting relationship wears off, that constraint can become increasingly problematic in the sexual part of a relationship. His partner, meanwhile, may have worked through early issues of denial and moved on in such a way that he is much more able to be exploratory. As the relationship progresses, they may have become more severely conflicted around the issue of spontaneity as opposed to constraints.

For long-term partners, this period tends to be one of instability, accompanied by a certain vibrancy, in that the practice of reevaluation, which may have been lost over a long period of togetherness and familiarity, offers an opportunity for a second chance at creating yet another map for remaining together. It also probably becomes clearer to people who are going through this stage that things never really do get settled. Partners in a reexamined relationship reach a reconciliation with the concept of stability and change, understanding that they are in constant flux. This no doubt happens in heterosexual relationships too, but I think it takes on a special meaning for gay couples because of the additional challenges of gay life. Gays finally understand, somehow, that as a person passes through these stages of development and his persona is consolidated, he begins to know better that stability and change are a constant part of his life. Uncertainty is a visitor he might just as well get comfortable with and deal with in a conscious manner.

Self-Partnering

In the heterosexual community there exists tremendous pressure for coupling, creating families, procreating—enough pressure, in fact, for the society to consider the decision to remain single much less desirable than the preferable way, or a choice that happens by default or failure, or a choice that raises suspicions of homosexuality.

Because the gay community honors and celebrates diversity, it looks much more benignly upon creating a life without a permanent partner, a life in which you partner yourself, so to speak, a lifestyle as equally viable as coupling. The tendency for this kind of man in the gay community is to create a chosen family that acts for him in the ways that a partner would act, in terms of trust, social and economic support, emotional support, and unconditional acceptance and belonging. As far as this family is concerned, he can do no wrong; they are his, he is theirs. His attachment is to them and not to his lover or lovers, whom he sees as transients in the pages of his biography.

He more than likely has developed in such a way as to treat himself the way he would treat a lover, with respect, kindness, and generosity. His sexual needs are likely to be satisfied in a series of continuous affairs or with a long-term sex buddy of a similar disposition, so that neither one is the other's primary attachment.

He is not a peripheral member of his gay family. In fact, he could be the leading member, equivalent to patriarch or matriarch, satisfying his nurturing self by presiding over the clan. He may satisfy his nurturing needs with a high level of involvement in gay community and political activities. Free as he is from the more time-consuming responsibilities of a full-time relationship, and growing older and wiser as an impartial observer of the personalities and relationships in all of his periphery, he may feel most fulfilled as a counselor, guide, or mentor.

Mentoring

Giving Back

Following a period of probing self-evaluation, however long that process takes, the adult gay man who has either changed his life or reconciled his position in it inevitably makes a commitment to life with new meaning and purpose, sometimes even with new energy for continued growth.

Having spent his lifetime breaking out of conventional patterns by virtue of his homosexuality, he now enters a period of deeper self-acceptance and contentment, one with greater tolerance for himself and others, probably with a decreasing tendency to compare himself with others and with a greater awareness of philosophical concerns.

Like his heterosexual counterpart, he enters this stage having to deal with the increasing health limitations that accompany aging; with adapting to or anticipating a string of losses, from his own physical attractiveness to the loss of position and power in his career and his society, to the deaths of partners and friends; and with the hope that if he chose to, he might be able to share the benefit of his life experiences to smooth the way of people who have yet to make the same passage.

The gay man seems to have an edge on aging well, especially in an age-prejudiced society. Many researchers suggest that as a result of what it means to be lesbian and gay in a heterosexist world, many gay men develop exceptional skills for managing their lives, which facilitate their adjustment to the aging process (John A. Lee, in *Gay Midlife and Maturity*).

Having achieved a life of integrity, the older gay man has learned to value himself, to depend on himself, to survive in the face of stigma. He already has learned to master societal rejection, and that knowledge will serve him as an age-prejudiced society turns its back on him, viewing him as less and less useful, competent, and valuable.

Heterosexual men who have had the protection of their families of origin and then their supportive families of procreation may not be as well prepared for the demands of aging, for dealing with changes like the departure of children, or reduced incomes that may require greater creativity for survival, changes like the loss of a partner or the deaths of friends.

The gay man has been dealing with the loss of friends and family since he began coming out to them and, to varying degrees, since the beginning of the AIDS epidemic. He knows by now how to mobilize the vast network of professional community support if he needs it yet again.

The gay man does not feel so seriously the loss of such institutional supports as he did not have them to begin with; nor in most cases does he feel the departure of grown children; nor does he question the certainty and the tradition of extended families whom he could count on to provide for him in his later years, writes Richard Friend in *Gay Midlife and Maturity*. He is more likely to have developed the skills and flexibility needed to master the emotional and practical requirements of growing older, and even to have planned for his future security. He is more likely to have replaced the support that he may not have had from his family of origin with a strong network of friends and a chosen family whose members tend to be reinforcing during his later years.

Unlike the heterosexual man, who upon losing his wife might be at a serious loss for taking care of his basic needs, the contemporary gay man, while suffering just as much emotionally, will be much less shocked by the demands of widowhood, both practically and emotionally. With his tremendous flexibility regarding gender roles, the gay man usually is just as capable as his partner in preparing the meals, folding the laundry, and managing the household finances.

Bill, in his early sixties, an extremely robust, dignified man with a delightfully traditional charm and social grace, grew up in a family of immigrants who through incredible hard work and determination built a small neighborhood store into a major chain. He credits his homosexuality with preparing him for all of the challenges of growing older successfully, an ironic advantage, he says, denied his heterosexual friends, who in their respective youths enjoyed the advantages of membership in the dominant society. "I think gay men are a lot more self-sufficient than straight men," he says. "Gay men have to make a living just like straight men, but they also have to keep a home. Most straight men rely on their wives to organize their family and social lives. Gay men depend on themselves. In a relationship, one man might do the housework or organize the social calendar, but in general there's an enormous amount of flexibility. It's like the sex gay men have; we switch roles a lot. The same kind of flexibility we express in sex occurs naturally in every aspect of our lives. For gay men, roles tend not to be exclusive. I can deal with my household as well as with work.

"Years ago, when I was in my twenties, I asked an older gay friend, who lived alone much of his life, 'What do you do if you get sick?' I was worried because, in my background, your mother would take care of you, or your wife, or your daughter. He answered, wisely, 'If you get sick, you go to the hospital.' Of course. You do what you have to do.

"Being gay has helped me a great deal in my life. For a gay man it's okay to feel someone's sorrow and want to help. We are not ashamed of our emotions. As a matter of fact, for me it's been one of the things that's been so soothing about being gay, that I feel safe about being tender and vulnerable. The gay world in general is not threatened by empathy. I've heard stories of young men who are taking care of their friends and lovers, ill with AIDS, in ways that their own families couldn't possibly do or know how to do. A gay man will go in and do what has to be done. It's this quality of nurturing that is so transforming and moves throughout the gay community from one nuclear circle outward.

"My mother once said to me, 'What are you going to do when you get older, if you don't have a wife? Who's going to take care of you?' I answered, 'There's no guarantee that anybody would take care of me, even if I was married.' I don't have a lover, and there are moments when I am lonely. But over the years I've learned to structure my life by planning activities with friends."

The mythological image of the lonely, sex-crazed older gay man does not accurately reflect the autumn of life for these men, who tend by this stage to lead quietly well-adjusted and satisfying lives, according to J. Kelly in his pioneering study "The Aging Male Homosexual." Most have traveled the long and difficult road toward self-acceptance—though here and there undoubtedly are those who came of age during the most oppressive times and may have so internalized society's negative views that they do behave the way they have been taught. For the most part, gay men growing up under circumstances in which there was no emotional support draw on their monumental strength and have found the self-validation that they've needed to survive. Since they have challenged negative stereotypes for their whole lives, they are in a perfect position to observe, gauge, and act on what might be the best way to assist younger or more fragile men in freeing themselves from their own struggles; to help nurture them through the invention of a vision of a satisfying life; to provide advice and instruction in helping them validate their own identities.

Jack, for instance, retired at fifty-eight involuntarily. An endlessly energetic man, animated and chatty, he has lived alone most of his life and with no institutional support. He developed a very strong independent life, from which emerged his stoic, do-it-yourself philosophy, punctuated by his never having taken a long-term lover. He also developed a strong family of friends for social and emotional support and then cultivated, over the past two decades, a form of mentoring that reflects his philosophy of life. He organizes events, occasions, parties, or benefits, and brings people together to benefit both the community and one another. He gets his satisfaction watching people network, couple, learn, and get help.

"I feel I create occasions," he says, "events for people to come together and solve their problems. They will pick up things from being around more experienced people. I certainly don't have all the answers, but I don't always realize what I do know either, and you never know what's going to come together for someone at one of these events."

Jack differed from others of his contemporaries whose style of mentoring was more personal and one-to-one regarding advice and counseling.

For a boy to become a man—just as for a girl to become a woman—he can profit from the active intervention of those who have made the passage, who have proven for themselves the wisdom of the earlier men and women who handed down the lessons of their own experiences. He, or she, may need and most likely would benefit from the older person to guide him through such rites of passage as are required for balanced development. The older gay man also deserves the respect and honor due his hard-earned achievements and his wealth of experience, and like the older heterosexual—man or woman—he wants to share them.

Without the benefits of their mutual contributions, that is, the older man's wisdom and the younger's ideological—and maybe physiological—generativeness, the future surely will suffer from isolation from the past and thus will guarantee the perpetuation of negative stereotypes, internalized loathing, and societal ostracism.

Oddly, in establishing himself as a mentor, the older gay man may have to navigate as much prejudice emanating from his own gay community as from the dominant society. In a society that favors youth, he lives in a subculture that has absolutely glorified youthful masculinity as a defense against society's feminized stereotyping. Within the subculture the older gay man historically has been ostracized for his diminishing attractiveness and his decreasing physical prowess. But with improving social conditions and greater acceptance comes the maturing of the gay community at large and the shift in value emphasis from body to soul. No phenomenon so graphically illustrates this emerging shift of emphasis among gays as the entire community's mobilization to fight the epidemic. Examples of mentoring and nurturing abound as the more experienced, ironically healthier older gay men, who usually are more financially secure, support their ill and dying brothers.

As a result, even in the gay community, preconceived notions about old gays are giving way to the more accurate, and frankly, the more logical, perception of these men as people who have had rich and rewarding lives and who with generosity and grace are willing to share the benefits of their experiences to help others.

"In the beginning of my gay life," says Bill, "when I came out in the early fifties, I in my early twenties, gay guys would ask, 'Who is your mother?' What people meant in those days by 'Who is your mother?' was 'Who is the person who brought you out?' Not the person who seduced you or who was the first to have sex with you, but the older, more experienced gay man who looked after you, who introduced you into the mysteries of gay life, into the language, into the culture, who educated you as to what was safe or wasn't safe. In those days what gay men were concerned about was navigating the harrowing social and sexual world of being gay. The dangers were very real then. You could get mixed up with the police with no trouble, or with someone who was exploitative, or rough trade, for that matter, who might steal from you or beat you up. At that time gay men were not so visible. People didn't know where to go to meet. The person who took care of you, who introduced you to all of that, you called your mother. I suppose because he was nurturing, and nurturing was considered a feminine trait. I still remember the person in my life who acted as my mother. My mentor, so to speak. He died in an accident some years back, and I was devastated.

"As I've gotten older, I've discovered that my values are very much like those of my father's, his sense of social responsibility, familial responsibility, personal integrity, helping other people who need help, whether it was financial, business advice, or emotional counsel. If someone was in a scrape, he would invariably help. He was an open-handed man, a limited man too, because he wasn't born here. He wasn't educated. He didn't understand the world that I was climbing into. He wouldn't have been able to deal with my heartache.

"Now that it isn't as difficult to be gay, at least in the same way, that kind of mentoring, the kind 'Mother' offered, is no longer necessary. The type of mentoring that I think people provide today concerns helping one get ahead, solving psychological problems, or counseling on questions on how to find or manage a relationship. But not advice on how to stay out of the hands of police or how to find gay people, because that's obvious now.

"I found myself doing many of the things my father did. But I also find myself helping people in ways he wasn't helpful. My father gave unlimited advice or practical help. I got paragraphs of what to do, but he couldn't really listen or hear my underlying problems. For decades I've navigated the difficulties of being gay, as well as those of life in general, and perhaps because my father was unable to listen, it's something I'm determined to do well with younger people who come to me with their problems. There are young people who come into the social groups I am part of, and I am aware that they need encouragement and they need praise, and they need to be told that they are doing a good job at whatever level they are functioning. I do for them what I vicariously would have wanted done for me.

"When I speak publicly at the gay synagogue, I never speak carelessly. I remind people of the fact that we are a group that has contributed in our own important way to communal life, that is, to both the gay community and society at large. I say we have to be proud of what we have accomplished, and what we have accomplished has been against a great many odds.

"The kind of mentoring I see gay men doing is not just in the professional arena by providing apprenticeships—as happens, say, among musicians. With gay people there's always the element of nurturing. Gay mentoring almost automatically includes emotional caretaking. And in that sense gay mentoring is not the same kind of mentoring that occurs in the various professional worlds."

I accepted an invitation to speak at NYU in April 1993 as part of a university-wide, month-long series of lectures and workshops celebrating homosexuality. The idea struck me as astoundingly forward-looking, given my vivid recollections of my first year of college at Columbia, when there seemed no possibility of gay men congregating.

Seventy-five to a hundred college students attended. Two-thirds of them were gay, the rest friends and siblings interested in what I had to say about the psychological development of their fellows, based on this work in progress.

I learned from the subsequent interaction that some of the gay members of the audience had been born into an environment so completely different from my own that I was almost a living relic, offering them a history of the struggle of their pioneer forebears. They had grown to young manhood on assumptions that I had struggled for decades to learn and accept. Their homosexuality was a reality they already had acknowledged and embraced. They were more interested in fine-tuning it, and I felt strongly I could learn more from them than they from me.

Others—and in significant numbers—clearly were struggling with the same questions, fears, and issues I had evaded in 1964 and then confronted so tortuously in the years chronicled in this book. Still, the amazing and encouraging difference was that they did have a peer population near them, identifiable, accessible, and eager to assist as they wrestled with their identities and whatever awful messages they had received and believed about themselves.

It was the straight population in the room that most impressed and encouraged me, exercising whatever brave intellectual curiosity and emotional courage it took even to attend such a lecture. It gave me hope. It reminded me of something I had just learned about my friend Margaret and her son at the Washington demonstration in 1987. Her son was wearing an Act Up T-shirt, the Silence = Death shirt, and she told me only recently that after our encounter there, a museum guard had spotted the boy's shirt and asked him tauntingly what the slogan meant. Margaret's son answered, "It's about AIDS. It's about people's rights." And then, after a boy's pause, he added: "If we don't stand up for people's rights, we'll all be dead."

Epilogue

The Closeted Homophobe

by Ed Lowe, Jr.

Kidnappers had seized a wealthy manufacturer named Jack Teich from his driveway in the Long Island community of Kings Point. For seven days in 1974 they kept him tied up in a closet, until his family delivered $750,000 in ransom.

During that week, in one of his compulsive daily telephone calls to an assistant editor at *Newsday*, New York novelist and newspaper personality Jimmy Breslin offered a suggestion for kidnap coverage, and his impressionable little friend took it quite seriously. Breslin cited two uptown bars that he insisted were regular daily watering holes for agents assigned to the New York office of the Federal Bureau of Investigation. He said *Newsday* should assign a reporter to one or both of the two bars after work hours to eavesdrop on agents who doubtless would be discussing the Teich kidnapping over drinks. Breslin was a columnist for the *Daily News* at the time.

Possibly because I was a saloonist, I drew the resulting assignment to drive from *Newsday*'s Nassau County offices into the city and loiter in the two taverns. I was not yet a columnist and had no business telling anybody what I thought of the idea.

In both bars, the jukeboxes played so homicidally loud, I had to order my beer by mime. Also, both bars were nearly empty. I could not have overheard such agents as were not present anyhow, even if they were shouting their secrets into my face.

Also, I could not telephone my news desk from either place to say how impossible and ridiculous was this assignment, because nobody would have heard me. In search of a quiet restaurant with a pay phone, I rounded a corner onto a wide avenue and spied an awning bearing the name COUPLES in script, superimposed over a logo consisting of two overlapping hearts sewn together by an arrow piercing both.

I was twenty-eight years old and deep in the throes of a failed first marriage. We had met when she was fifteen and I seventeen and just three weeks removed from a preparatory seminary whose administrator, a monsignor, had correctly deduced that I did not have a divine vocation to the priesthood.

Perhaps I could salvage this evening, I thought as I misinterpreted the Couples logo, by making my phone call from a place where I could also steal a look at some pretty New York women.

Through two sets of heavy brass and glass doors, I pushed into the East River dark of Couples. Ahead of me and slightly to the left, I could make out the portly bartender's white shirt and apron, the only objects visible. Upon our convergence at the elbow of the bar, I asked the bartender for a bottle of Budweiser and directions to the pay phone. I don't recall what he said in response, but I do recall that in saying it, he raised his brow and half closed his eyes, which fluttered as he spoke. My eyes were just becoming accustomed to the darkness. His high voice, his fluid bearing, and his petulant tone blended uneasily with my growing awareness of the attention focused on me by the other patrons at the bar, all of them, now that I looked, male.

In the irrationally stereotyped snapshots of my memory, all the men were slender too, and clad in silk shirts. All had languidly draped one leg over the other. All were paired and arranged contiguously.

I did not know the word *homophobia* at the time, but obviously it fueled my chain of involuntary neurological responses.

New York prices being what they were, I managed to guzzle the entire beer before I hastened to the doors, stage-mumbling about not having enough time to make the phone call after all. I seized the brass door handle on the right side and yanked it once. It resisted. A sudden shot of adrenaline inspired me to yank a second time, harder. The door resisted still. A young man's voice drifted out from a darkened coatroom to my left. With amused exasperation he said: "The left. The door on the left."

I thanked him, grasped the handle to my left, leaned back like a water skier on one ski, opened the door, thrust myself to the second set of doors, and escaped to the sidewalk, where I immediately made eye contact with a businessman strolling by.

"Wrong place!" I said, excusing myself to a stranger for a perceived mistake he neither knew nor cared about. "Wrong place," I repeated, smiling dumbly, hoping for a knowing grin in return. "That's the wrong place." The man looked at me, showing no change in expression. I turned left and strode north, behind him. As I reached the corner, the longest, widest Mercedes I had ever seen sped across my path and pulled to a stop beneath a sign that forbade parking until after 7:00 P.M. weekdays. Six well-dressed men got out and headed back across the street, straight for Couples. I stood at the curb, watching them, as agape as a small boy at a fireman's funeral.

Years later, I wondered why my reaction to the sudden realization that I was in a gay bar would be so pathetically exaggerated, and what were its origins, and whether I was more afraid of being among homosexual men or of being seen among them and thought to be one. But immediately afterward I did not ponder such questions at all. In fact, I remained complacently comfortable about my homophobia, a secure participant, I suppose, in a passive sort of mob rule, not very unlike the rule of the more insidious American racist, silently noticing the atrocities of a system whose unfair advantages he blithely accepts daily— occasionally disgusted with or ashamed of himself but always inert. I even retold the Couples story with a successfully entertaining, self-deprecating pride, as if in its humor my irrational terror provided solid evidence of my heterosexuality and therefore my acceptability, my membership in the dominant majority.

As a recovering Irish Catholic struggling halfheartedly and with mediocre success against my own racism, sexism, homophobia, and my fear of someday having to learn to speak Spanish, I am an unseen villain of this book, as are most of the kids I grew up with, hung out with, studied with, worked with, raised children with, and became middle-aged with, as are almost all their parents and, unfortunately, many of their children. I am more embarrassed than ashamed at the discovery, and I am not proud of the confession. I do wonder why so simple, obvious, and profound a character flaw would have escaped not just my notice but that of nearly everybody I know or have known. There must be such overwhelming comfort in ostracizing, a feeling of safety and belonging so powerful that it erases the instinct for compassion and substitutes cruelty in even the kindest souls.

The first time I met Stanley Siegel, he was a practicing family therapist who also was writing a *Newsday* column on families and family relationships. I soon learned that he was married and the father of a daughter, that he was smart, soft-spoken, and possessed of the sartorial taste of a fashion editor.

In contrast, I dressed like a clam digger reluctantly attending the funeral of a cousin once removed. Siegel and I were from polar opposite backgrounds, but each liked the way the other thought, and we seemed to share a fundamental optimism about our species that was rare among New Yorkers and nearly non-existent among New York journalists (and, I have long suspected, psychotherapists).

I was intrigued and inspired by Siegel's deftness at viewing people and their relationships from a perspective that became painfully obvious only after he suggested it and that always seemed to be giving the individual "the benefit of the doubt," a phrase my policeman father had employed mantra-like as a rule for each personal encounter in his life.

Following our initial acquaintanceship, I did not see Stanley Siegel for ten years. When I met him again, he was an openly gay man, living with his gay partner, and I was somewhat surprised that it seemed to make no difference to me, though I don't know what I might have expected. My homophobia had abated slightly with the decade and some assimilated enlightenment from the literature of my generation. In all that time, though, despite my journeyman status in a craft where gays are not at all uncommon, I still had been a guest in a gay home only once in my life. Even then I was merely a guest's husband/escort, and an uncomfortable one at that. The few gay men I knew always were delightful company, but I probably would not have invited any of them to accompany me to one of the saloons I frequented—not that they would have accepted such an invitation.

The first Siegel/Lowe project was our collaborating on *The Patient Who Cured His Therapist*, a book of stories taken from Siegel's files and videotapes following twenty years of practicing what he liked to call his art, psychotherapy. I entered into the project on a handshake, swathed in emotional and intellectual ignorance about gay culture or just about any information pertaining to gays, but never guessing that the subject might come up during the writing of the book. However, two of the thirteen stories involved gay men, and one story required my describing the affection and devotion two gay lovers communicated to each other nonverbally, while one of them was dying of AIDS. I worried that I might be unable to do it.

Through a series of conversations in which I interviewed Siegel as if either he or I were from an alien culture, I learned to accept both intellectually and emotionally two very simple truths about homosexuality: that a gay man is homosexual in the way I am right-handed or brown-eyed, and that therefore the way he feels when he is attracted, infatuated, or in love is analogous to the way I feel under similar circumstances toward a member of the opposite gender. Prior to the acceptance of these elementary notions, whenever I tried to "give the benefit of the doubt" to homosexuality and not think or feel prejudicially about gays, my imagination stopped dead short at the notion of my being sexually engaged with another man. I could not imagine it. I literally shuddered at the thought, and then probably tacitly condemned all homosexual men as crazy or sick for being able to imagine it themselves.

In the incalculable arrogance of the heterosexist, I had been trying to gauge how I would feel in Siegel's shoes without actually imagining myself wearing them. I was trying to imagine how I, a heterosexual man, could become sexually attracted to another man. I am not homosexual, so the thought was unnatural to me. Once I accepted that Siegel's stimulus-response system was identical to mine but for the gender of the stimulus; once I imagined him as programmed differently but otherwise built on the exact same plan; once I realized that his reactions to an attractive man were as natural to him as mine were to an attractive woman, I could re-create his recollection of the two gay lovers from my own vividly remembered heterosexual experiences. It was so simple a step, I felt abysmally ignorant for not having taken it before. The results were simple too, mere descriptions of ordinary human contact like: "The two touched frequently—pats on the shoulder, gentle hand clasps, Tyrone brushing Martin's thinned hair behind his ears or away from his forehead, Martin reaching out and resting his bony palm on Tyrone's forearm, thigh or shoulder."

During the writing of *The Patient Who Cured His Therapist*, Siegel talked more frequently about his need to chronicle his personal journey and write a book that would both describe and celebrate the psychological development of a gay male in the hostile environment of a society that routinely and universally condemned him, despite his exiled culture's enormous and courageous contributions to the same larger society. Also during the writing of the book, Siegel and I became good friends.

In addition to being Irish Catholic, I also was raised a Brooklyn Dodger fan, which forged my passionate longing for the triumph of the underdog, particularly the institutionalized underdog, against not only all odds but every cruel effort of the disproportionately enfranchised as well.

So, a month after we finished the first book, we began writing the second.

When *Uncharted Lives* was more than half finished, Siegel fell into a love affair that we later included in the autobiographical narrative. During the alternating euphoria and misery of that period, when his loyalties and passions were being stretched beyond their limits and his heart broken weekly, I served as his adviser and counselor, constantly reaching back for all that I had learned and much that I evidently had not learned in my romantic relationships with women, including two faded-away marriages. I'd come a long way from trying to bolt out of Couples in fear of . . . nothing in particular.

I expect that a gay audience will read, understand, benefit from, and applaud *Uncharted Lives*. I hope, though, that their fathers, mothers, siblings, and straight friends read this book and siphon such wisdom as they can from my efforts to comprehend, filter, and translate what I have learned during this collaboration.

Index